2004

W9-CLF-753

Human Diversity in Action

Developing Multicultural Competencies for the Classroom

Second Edition

Kenneth Cushner
Kent State University

McGraw Hill

Boston   Burr Ridge, IL   Dubuque, IA   Madison, WI   New York   San Francisco   St. Louis
Bangkok   Bogotá   Caracas   Kuala Lumpur   Lisbon   London   Madrid   Mexico City
Milan   Montreal   New Delhi   Santiago   Seoul   Singapore   Sydney   Taipei   Toronto

McGraw-Hill Higher Education

A Division of The McGraw-Hill Companies

HUMAN DIVERSITY IN ACTION: DEVELOPING MULTICULTURAL COMPETENCIES FOR THE CLASSROOM
Kenneth Cushner

Published by McGraw-Hill, an imprint of The McGraw-Hill Companies, Inc., 1221 Avenue of the Americas, New York, NY 10020. Copyright © 2003 (2000) by The McGraw-Hill Companies, Inc. All rights reserved. No part of this publication may be reproduced or distributed in any form or by any means, or stored in a database or retrieval system, without the prior written consent of The McGraw-Hill Companies, Inc., including, but not limited to, in any network or other electronic storage or transmission, or broadcast for distance learning.

1 2 3 4 5 6 7 8 9 0 BKM/BKM 0 9 8 7 6 5 4 3 2 1

ISBN 0-07-248881-6

www.mhhe.com

About the Author

Kenneth Cushner (Ed. D.) is Associate Dean for Student Life and Intercultural Affairs and Professor in the College and Graduate School of Education at Kent State University. He is a frequent contributor to the professional literature in multicultural and intercultural education and is internationally known for his work in the professional development of educators through workshops and consultation. Among his publications, Dr. Cushner is the author or co-author of *Human Diversity in Education: An Integrative Approach, 4/e* (McGraw-Hill, 2003), *International Perspectives on Intercultural Education (Lawrence Erlbaum Associates, 1998); Intercultural Interactions: A Practical Guide, 2/e* (Sage Publications, 1996), and *Improving Intercultural Interactions: Modules for Cross-Cultural Training Programs, Volume 2* (Sage Publications, 1997). Dr. Cushner has developed and led international travel programs on all seven continents. In his spare time, Dr. Cushner enjoys music (percussion and guitar), travel and photography.

I've often thought there ought to be a manual to hand to little kids, telling them what kind of planet they're on, why they don't fall off, how much time they've probably got here, how to avoid poison ivy, and so on. . . .And one thing I would really like to tell them about is cultural relativity. I didn't learn until I was in college about all the other cultures, and I should have learned that in the first grade. A first grader should understand that his or her culture isn't a rational invention; that there are thousands of other cultures and they all work pretty well; that all cultures function on faith rather than truth; that there are lots of alternatives to our own society. Cultural relativity is defensible and attractive. It's also a source of hope. It means we don't have to continue this way if we don't like it.

Kurt Vonnegut
1974, p. 139

Perhaps this is the start of that manual.

Kenneth Cushner 2002

v

Table of Contents

Part II   Getting to Know the Culture of Others: Intercultural Interaction

Part III   Modifying Curriculum and Instruction to Address the Goals of Diversity

Preface

The world continues to become so interdependent that the smooth functioning of many governments, economies and businesses demand that individuals have awareness, knowledge and the skill to interact effectively with others whose cultures may be quite different from their own. This has become especially evident to most of us in light of the events of September 11, 2001. It is increasingly clear that people must strive to better understand those who are culturally different as well as to make themselves better known to others. This will be no simple feat given what we know about the manner in which people learn about others.

The Purpose of this Workbook

The fields of cross-cultural training and intercultural education have grown remarkably in the past decades in response to these very real needs. One thing that stands out in the research in the field of intercultural education and training is the critical role that experience plays in culture learning. That is, while it is relatively easy to transfer a significant amount of sound information to others through cognitive approaches such as lectures, books and films, little of this information results in new behavior on the part of students and trainees. Thus, typical multicultural courses that emphasize lecture and readings may fall far short of achieving the very goals they set out to accomplish; students and teachers just do not become more effective in their interpersonal interactions or in modifying their instruction simply by being presented with new information. Rather, people learn to live and work more effectively with others as a result of long-term immersion and experiences that engage the emotions, and often precede or accompany cognitive inputs.

This workbook was developed with the intent of providing the student of culture with structured experiences designed to increase one's awareness, knowledge and skill in intercultural understanding and interaction with the ultimate impact being upon teachers and students in schools. Through this workbook, students and instructors can become actively engaged in a number practical exercises that examine critical elements of the educational process that are influenced by culture. They can then discuss their experiences with others, thus learning the benefit of reflection, dialogue and collaboration.

To the Instructor: Using the Workbook

This workbook will be useful to those teaching a variety of courses where cultural and/or human diversity are central elements. People have found these exercises to be of value in such courses as multicultural or intercultural education, global or international education, social studies or other methods courses that require students to attend to diversity in very real ways, new student orientation courses that emphasize diversity issues, as well as in a variety of field experience settings, including student teaching seminar. It is also a very useful addition to the professional development of practicing teachers, providing the workshop consultant with a variety of activities designed to bring aspects of diversity to the forefront.

This workbook can easily accompany the fourth edition of *Human Diversity in Education: An Integrative Approach*, (Cushner, McClelland and Safford, McGraw-Hill, 2003), and workbook activities are keyed directly in the text at appropriate points to alert students and instructors. The workbook can also be used on its own, or can easily be used as a complement to many of the multicultural textbooks currently available on the market. **An accompanying correlation chart identifies where specific activities might be used in conjunction with some of the other multicultural textbooks that are in current use. The correlation chart is available at www.mhhe.com/cushner4e in the** *Human Diversity in Action* **section.**

To the Student: Using the Workbook

It is important that you recognize that in order to truly understand diversity and issues surrounding culture that you must be an active participant. Culture learning is not effectively accomplished in a passive mode. This workbook is, thus, designed to be consumable, and is intended to be linked closely with the content you are reading about in your textbook. You are encouraged to write in this workbook and to use the various exercises as guides to help you develop a more culturally-sensitive approach to your interactions with others, and ultimately a more authentic approach to teaching and learning.

Online Resources

Resources for the workbook are housed at www.mhhe.com/cushner4e under *Human Diversity in Action*. indicates that the activity can be done online. Also available online are relevant Web links.

The Organization of the Workbook

This workbook provides a number of exercises that are presented in three different sections, or levels of culture learning. Part I provides some basic content related to the concept of culture and the development of self. It is essential that anyone seriously interested in exploring the complex phenomenon of culture and intercultural interaction look closely at the various dynamics that have gone into the formation of self. Part II provides some basic frameworks and skills in the analysis of cultural differences and the processes involved in intercultural interaction. Part III presents exercises to provide insight into culture's influence on teaching and learning as well as a number of strategies that can be used to modify existing curriculum and instruction. You are encouraged to use these exercises over a relatively long period of time, such as throughout a semester or academic year, as the changes that we are all required to make, both within ourselves as well as within our institutions, are quite dramatic and will not happen overnight.

New to the Second Edition

This second edition of the workbook follows a similar format as the first edition. There are some changes to the current edition, however, that are based on the feedback of a number of the current users. For instance, an Inventory of Cross-Cultural Sensitivity has been added, both early in the book as well as toward the end. This inventory can be used as a pre-post assessment as well as to set the context for some of the major concepts that are to be covered throughout the book. Guidelines for journal writing are also introduced earlier in this edition. There are also a number of new exercises that have been developed to both broaden as well as further expand the scope of the coverage. New exercises address issues related to language learning, bias and the formation of stereotypes, privilege, a community scan, as well as intercultural interaction. In addition, the format for the critical incidents has been modified, with the responses for all of them now located at the end of the section. Also new are objectives for each activity, key terms included in the glossary, the Correlation Chart to key activities to other multicultural textbooks, and the addition of Web links.

Acknowledgements

A project such as this cannot develop and improve without the insights and assistance of a number of individuals. To this end, the following individuals deserve thanks:

Gary Stephen Allison, University of Delaware

Barrie A. Brancato, Clarion University of Pennsylvania

Reyna G. Garcia Ramos, Pepperdine University

Dr. Joyce Gibson, University of Massachusetts, Lowell

Judith A. Hakes, Angelo State University

JoAnn Parla, SUNY Fredonia

Susan Peters, Michigan State University

Otilia Salmon, University of North Florida

Dr. Rosemary F. Schiavi, Loras College

part one

Getting to Know the Culture of Self

 Go to www.mhhe.com/cushner4e and click on *Human Diversity in Action* for a listing of Web Links.

Mental Maps of Culture: An Icebreaker

Purpose

1. To provide an opportunity for you to reflect upon your early experiences related to culture and intercultural interaction.

2. To learn about others as you each share and discuss your early experiences and understanding of the concept of culture

Instructions

Reflect upon some of the experiences you had growing up that may have influenced your understanding of the concept of culture. Perhaps you grew up in an environment that was filled with culturally diverse experiences and encounters. Or, perhaps you were raised in a rather segregated or protected environment and had little direct experience with people different from yourself. When did you first learn about different people? How did you react to this experience? What messages did others give you – either intentionally or not, that you still remember today? How have you come to understand the concept of culture today? Reflect back over your life and try to recall events and experiences along the way that have influenced your feelings and thoughts about people from different cultural backgrounds.

In the space below, or on another sheet of paper, make a drawing or diagram that includes your experiences and your thoughts, feelings and understandings related to culture. Then, using your drawing, introduce yourself to one or two other people while sharing your experiences around culture. In your discussion, look for similarities and differences in your feelings and thoughts, the events and experiences that contributed to their development, and the people who influenced you along the way.

Inventory of Cross-Cultural Sensitivity

©Kenneth Cushner,
1986

Purpose

To complete a self-assessment instrument with regard to your intercultural experiences.

Instructions:

The following questionnaire asks you to rate your agreement or disagreement with a series of statements. Please respond honestly as there are no correct answers. You will find another copy of this in the last section of the workbook that you can complete toward the end of the course. You can compare your responses from the beginning to the end of the book.

Please circle the number that best corresponds to your level of agreement with each statement below

	1 = Strongly Disagree 7 = Strongly Agree
1. I speak only one language	1…2…3…4…5…6…7
2. The way other people express themselves is very interesting to me	1…2…3…4…5…6…7
3. I enjoy being with people from other cultures	1…2…3…4…5…6…7
4. Foreign influence in our country threatens our national identity	1…2…3…4…5…6…7
5. Other's feelings rarely influence decisions I make	1…2…3…4…5…6…7
6. I can not eat with chopsticks	1…2…3…4…5…6…7
7. I avoid people who are different from me	1…2…3…4…5…6…7
8. It is better that people from other cultures avoid one another	1…2…3…4…5…6…7
9. Culturally mixed marriages are wrong	1…2…3…4…5…6…7

	1 = Strongly Disagree *7 = Strongly Agree*
10. I think people are basically alike	1...2...3...4...5...6...7
11. I have never lived outside my own culture for any great length of time	1...2...3...4...5...6...7
12. I have foreigners to my home on a regular basis	1...2...3...4...5...6...7
13. It makes me nervous to talk to people who are different from me	1...2...3...4...5...6...7
14. I enjoy studying about people from other cultures	1...2...3...4...5...6...7
15. People from other cultures do things differently because they do not know any other way	1...2...3...4...5...6...7
16. There is usually more than one good way to get things done	1...2...3...4...5...6...7
17. I listen to music from another culture on a regular basis	1...2...3...4...5...6...7
18. I decorate my home or room with artifacts from other countries	1...2...3...4...5...6...7
19. I feel uncomfortable when in a crowd of people	1...2...3...4...5...6...7
20. The very existence of humanity depends upon our knowledge about other people	1...2...3...4...5...6...7
21. Residential neighborhoods should be culturally separated	1...2...3...4...5...6...7
22. I have many friends	1...2...3...4...5...6...7
23. I dislike eating foods from other cultures	1...2...3...4...5...6...7
24. I think about living within another culture in the future	1...2...3...4...5...6...7
25. Moving into another culture would be easy	1...2...3...4...5...6...7
26. I like to discuss issues with people from other cultures	1...2...3...4...5...6...7
27. There should be tighter controls on the number of immigrants allowed into my country	1...2...3...4...5...6...7
28. The more I know about people, the more I dislike them	1...2...3...4...5...6...7
29. I read more national news than international news in the daily newspaper	1...2...3...4...5...6...7
30. Crowds of foreigners frighten me	1...2...3...4...5...6...7

	1 = Strongly Disagree 7 = Strongly Agree
31. When something newsworthy happens I seek out someone from that part of the world to discuss the issue with	1...2...3...4...5...6...7
32. I eat ethnic foods at least twice a week	1...2...3...4...5...6...7

Scoring the ICCS

The ICCS can be scored by subscales. Simply insert the number circled on the test form in the spaces provided under each subscale heading. Reverse the values for the items marked with an asterisk (*). For instance, reverse scoring results in:

$$7=1,\ 6=2,\ 5=3,\ 4=4,\ 3=5,\ 2=6,\ 1=7$$

Then, add the values in each column for the subscale score. A total ICCS score is obtained by adding the various subscale scores together. Individuals can be ranked relative to others in a particular group. You can also identify relative strengths and weaknesses that may lead to more focused orientation and planning.

ICCS Scoring Guide   Subject ID_____

C Scale		*B Scale*		*I Scale*	
item	score	item	score	item	score
1*	____	2	____	3	____
6*	____	7*	____	8*	____
11*	____	13*	____	14	____
12	____	19*	____	20	____
17	____	25*	____	26	____
18	____	30	____	31	____
23*	____				
24	____				
29*	____				
32	____				

	A Scale		E Scale	
	item	*score*	*item*	*score*
	4*	____	5*	____
	9*	____	10	____
	15*	____	16	____
	21*	____	22	____
	27*	____	28*	____

Totals

C Scale = ____

B Scale = ____

I Scale = ____

A Scale = ____

E Scale = ____

Total ICCS Score = ____

* Reverse score all items marked with * as these are negatively worded items.

Interpreting the Inventory of Cross-Cultural Sensitivity

The ICCS is a 32-item instrument composed of five subscales that provides dimensional scores for individuals on each subscale. Individuals can be ranked relative to others from high to low levels of sensitivity on issues and experiences related to cross-cultural or intercultural interaction (the higher the score, the more sensitive an individual is presumed to be). Results of such an inventory are of potential interest to those who need to identify individuals best able to under-take an international or intercultural transfer or those best able to adjust to the demands of cross-cultural personnel changes (e.g. desegregation efforts in schools); programs that desire to evaluate the impact of curriculum intervention and program experience; and for those wishing to simply raise people's aware-ness of some of the issues to consider prior to intercultural interaction. (The technical details of the ICCS can be found following the ICCS in Part 3.)

The five subscales and the range of scores include:

Subscale	Range of Scores
Cultural Integration (C Scale)	10–70
Behavioral Scale (B Scale)	6–42
Intellectual Interaction (I Scale)	6–42
Attitude Toward Others (A Scale)	5–35
Empathy Scale (E Scale)	5–35
Total Score Range	32–224

How did you do on the various subscales? In what areas are you strongest? Weakest?

_____

_____

_____

What might you do to improve on each of these scores?

_____

_____

_____

_____

Interpreting One's Own Intercultural Experience: The Magic of Journal Writing

(from an exercise developed by J. E. Rash, Legacy International)

Purpose

To develop the skills of documentation and reflection as you engage in the process of culture learning.

Instructions

One of the main purposes of this workbook is to provide you with a structure that enables you to engage in and analyze your intercultural interactions. One way to gain expertise in living and working across cultures is to broaden your base of experience while keeping a journal of your encounters. You can begin to do this by making regular visits to a "culturally-different" place in which you are initially not known. You should make these visits regularly over an extended period of time — say once or twice a week for two or three months. Some culturally-different places you might visit include a place of worship different from your own, a soup kitchen or homeless shelter, a school in an area that differs from one you are familiar with, a community group in another part of town, or a campus organization for a group you may not normally not attend (international student group, gay/lesbian student group, etc.). Begin simply by observing those around you. Document your initial feelings, emotional reactions, the assumptions you make, and the questions you have. After some time, check out your assumptions by interviewing some of the people you have observed and interacted with in the group. Ask for clarification of behavior or conversations that are still unclear. Reflect upon how the feelings, emotional reactions, assumptions, and questions you have may change over time. You may find the following guidelines helpful in organizing a journal.

Journal Writing

Personal culture learning can be more easily facilitated by keeping a journal of your observations, thoughts, reactions, and conclusions throughout your experiences with different groups. A journal will enable you to accomplish several objectives, including:

1. assisting you in developing and/or refining your skills in observation, reflection, and interpretation;
2. providing you with a record of your observations and activities, thus making it easier for you to prepare formal reports and presentations; and
3. providing you a basis for discussion and further reflection, should you decide to share some of your entries with others. Such an effort may help you to better understand the outcomes of your experiences.

The word "education," meaning "to lead forth" or to "draw out," includes both that which "comes in" to you as well as that which is "drawn out" from within you. As such, the journal is designed to help you account for the various levels of your learning, and is more than a step-by-step account of the experiences that you have each day or the emotional responses to those encounters. While your personal experiences and reactions are necessary, your journal will be a more useful tool if it also contains the personal reflections and learnings you encounter, written with a larger audience in mind. You are producing a piece that others may read and benefit from. These levels, or steps that should be included in your journal include:

Observation — What you perceive and/or what you experience;

Reflection — How you understand what you experience and perceive;

Translation — What you do with what you have learned, and how you relate what you have learned from one experience to others in your life; and,

Application — How you apply what you have learned in your personal and professional activities.

Your journal should include *at least* the following:

- What you experienced or observed;
- Your immediate reactions, thoughts, and feelings;
- Any further thoughts, feelings, ideas, or conclusions you have gained by reflecting on your observations and reactions;
- A review of your learning from the day;
- How you might transfer what you have learned to your life;
- Events, quotes, conversations, etc. you might want to include in your future presentations and reports.

You might ask yourself the following questions as you prepare your journal entry:

Observation — What one event, thought, conversation, etc. stood out in my mind today?

What was it about the event that made it stand out?

What about that event was significant?

Reflection — What have I learned about the thoughts, feelings, attitudes of children, teachers, or parents through this experience?

Have my thoughts changed?

What do I think about it now?

Have I learned something about myself by observing my thoughts?

Translation — What have I learned about the situation in the school?

In the community? In the lives of the children involved?

How can I apply what I have learned to my personal or professional life?

Other areas of investigation and observation you may wish to consider, especially when doing observations in schools include:

- Cultural differences and common factors among various groups and subgroups represented in the school;
- Teaching styles that seem to predominate in this classroom and in the school;
- Interpersonal interactions between students and teachers, students and students, teachers and teachers, teachers and administrators, parents and staff, etc.

A c t i v i t y   a n d   R e a d i n g   4

The Nature of Culture and Culture Learning

Purpose

To identify qualities that characterizes the concept of culture.

Instructions

Read and review the following material. Respond accordingly in the space provided.

The process by which we all come to believe that there is a "right" way to think, express ourselves, and act — in other words, how we learn our culture, is called **socialization**. It is the process by which individuals learn what is required of them in order to be successful members of a given group, whatever that group may be. Socialization is a unique process in that it simultaneously looks to the future and the past. It looks forward to where people are expected to be and backward to determine what behaviors, values, and beliefs are important to continue.

Socialization is such a potent process that people, once they have been socialized, are hardly aware that other realities can exist. This results in the presence of **ethnocentrism**, the tendency people have to judge others from their own culture's perspective, believing theirs to be the "right" or "correct" way to perceive and act within the world.

Most people in today's industrialized societies can be considered to be multicultural because they have been socialized by a number of different individuals or groups that influence their behavior and thought patterns (e.g., gender, nationality, ethnicity, social class, religion, and so forth. There is a more in-depth discussion of these later in the handbook.) At this point, it may be helpful to look at how culture, in the broadest sense, influences people's behavior. Brislin (2000) and Cushner and Brislin (1996) offer a discussion of features that are helpful in understanding culture's influence on behavior and that can be applied to the multiple influences suggested above. This list is summarized below, and readers are advised to apply it to the various groups with which they interact.

1. **Culture usually refers to something that is made by human beings rather than something that occurs in nature.**

   That is, when you look out over a large river basin, for instance, neither the trees and plants along the riverside, the water in the river, the land along the riverbank, nor the horizon are generally considered to be a part of culture. These are naturally-occurring components of the environment. However, if you look a little closer, and if you consider how people *think about* and what they *do* with the natural environment, then we can see culture's influence.

   Consider, for example, the Mississippi River or Nile River valleys. In various places along these riverbeds you will find numerous waterfront dwellings, perhaps a number of piers, many different kinds of boats, certainly a smattering of litter, and a range of farmland along the river's edge. This is all a part of the local culture and is likely to differ in many respects, according to the particular river being considered. But in addition, these products of culture also represent people's attitudes toward the natural environment. Thus human culture and the natural environment are always connected, usually in a variety of ways. In this instance, culture consists of interrelated components of material artifacts (the dwellings and boats), social and behavioral patterns (we have waste and we toss it in the water), and mental products (it's "all right" to toss litter in the water because somehow, the water will take care of it, and anyway, there's a lot of water).

2. **The most critical dimension of culture concerns itself with people's assumptions about life that are often unspoken or hidden from consciousness.**

   Culture includes the ideals, values, and assumptions about life that are widely shared and that guide specific behaviors. Triandis (1972) introduced us to the differences between objective and subjective culture. **Objective culture** refers to the visible, tangible elements of a culture, and may include such things as the artifacts people make, the food they eat, the clothing they wear, and even the names given to things. It is relatively easy to pick up, analyze, and hypothesize about the use and meaning of objective elements of culture.

   Subjective culture, on the other hand, refers to the invisible, less tangible aspects of a group of people, and includes such things as people's values, attitudes, norms of behavior, and the roles they adopt. It is often very difficult to verbalize elements of subjective culture as these things generally occur in people's minds. Most people lack the necessary vocabulary and have little practice speaking about aspects of subjective culture. It is thought that most problems people experience in cross-cultural communication occur at this level, and that good multicultural or cross-cultural training should focus on the subjective aspects of people's culture.

In this respect, and in rather simplistic terms, culture can be likened to an iceberg where only 10 percent of the whole is seen above the surface of the water. This visible portion is not what worries a ship's captain. It is the 90 percent of the iceberg that is hidden beneath the surface of the water that is of concern and is most likely to inflict damage to a ship. Like an iceberg, the most meaningful (and potentially dangerous) part of culture is the invisible or subjective part that is continually operating at the unconscious level to shape

**CULTURE,
LIKE AN ICEBERG,
HAS TWO DIMENSIONS**

**Objective culture — a surface layer
(artifacts, food, clothing)**

**and, Subjective culture — a deep dimension
(attitudes, values, beliefs)**

Figure 4-1

people's perceptions and responses to those perceptions. It is this aspect of culture that leads to most intercultural misunderstandings. Good intercultural understanding will enable people to develop a greater understanding of the hidden, or subjective, elements of another's culture, and thus make it easier to navigate the oftentimes muddy waters of cross-cultural interaction.

3. **Another common feature of culture is that it is a collective creation.**

That is, people construct culture through their social interactions with others. Cultural ideas are shared by a group of people who recognize the knowledge, attitudes, and values of one another. These people also agree on which cultural elements are to be adhered to and followed. Culture, then, is transmitted across generations by such people as parents, teachers, respected elders and religious leaders, and is mediated through a variety of sources, including the media, the stories parents tell their children, and the various experiences one has in a given culture's institutions and schools.

4. **There exist clear childhood experiences that individuals can identify that help to develop and teach particular values and practices.**

Among many in the middle class in the United States (and particularly among certain ethnic groups), individualism and self-reliance are strongly valued. If such a statement is generally accepted as indicative of an expression of one's culture, one should be able to identify specific examples from people's childhood experiences that help to develop such traits. Many people who grew up in the United States can remember having early jobs (paper routes, fast-food restaurants, baby-sitting) and proverbs that were influential ("God helps those who help themselves"; "The early bird catches the worm") that would help them develop individuality.

On the contrary, people of some ethnic or cultural backgrounds strongly value interdependence and a collective orientation, or a strong group identity. Examples of their early childhood experiences that might have direct influence on this value might include decision-making which was strongly influenced by one or more parents or other extended family members, and having early work experiences in a family owned and operated business. Proverbs such as "An acorn doesn't fall far from the tree," or "Without family, one is naked" all help to develop this collective orientation.

5. **Aspects of one's culture that guide behavior are not frequently spoken about.**

Much of one's culture is a secret even from oneself. People, generally, do not talk about their own culture since it is so widely shared and accepted as 'normal' and 'natural.' There just is little reason to discuss something that everyone seems to take for granted. As a result, people generally do not have an extensive vocabulary nor considerable practice discussing such issues when cross-cultural problems emerge. It thus becomes a major responsibility of cross-cultural trainers and multicultural educators to help individuals develop categories and a vocabulary that enables them to freely discuss the encounters they are experiencing, thus empowering them to resolve problems before they get out of hand.

6. **People are often uncomfortable or unable to discuss culture with others because there is often a lack of common vocabulary with a common meaning and understanding. Cultural differences, then, become most evident in well-meaning clashes.**

When people from two different cultures interact in ways that are proper and appropriate *from their perspective* but are different from that which is expected by the other, a complex series of events may unfold. What often happens is that when people confront differences with which they are unfamiliar, because they lack both an outsider's perspective on the elements of their own culture and a vocabulary with which to discuss that culture, they are unable to speak easily with others about the situation. While people may not be knowledgeable about what is happening between two people of different cultures, they are aware, on the emotional level, that things may not be right. People may become quite frustrated, may make negative judgments about others, and then may end an interaction at this point of frustration. In the worst-case scenario, people may continue to avoid those different from themselves due to the emotional discomfort that is present. Such a response must be avoided if productive encounters are to result. A major goal of good cross-cultural or multicultural education is to help people develop a vocabulary of related terms that they can begin to utilize in their interactions with others, thus establishing the groundwork for more effective communication, understanding, and problem resolution.

7. Culture allows people to provide important missing information and fill in the blanks, so to speak.

People who share common knowledge and who are in agreement about many cultural elements can communicate a considerable amount of information by sharing just a few words or phrases. For instance, when someone from work suggests that the office have a pot-luck lunch it is clear that this will consist of everyone bringing in a small dish of food to share with others. Notice that there is probably no expectation that people will receive a formal invitation, or that people will go home to change clothes and prepare a fancy dish. Nor is there the expectation that people will bring alcohol or make an entire afternoon of the activity. These are the gaps in people's knowledge that need not be spoken of and are commonly shared by others in the group. Outsiders to this group or culture may not be privy to the same, unspoken rules that are at play.

8. Cultural values tend to remain in practice, even in spite of compromises or slip-ups.

For instance, even though most people would agree that all should have fair and equal treatment under the law and a right to a fair and impartial trial, it is quite clear that the more wealthy and socially connected a person is, the easier it is to gain access to more powerful lawyers whose tactics may result in a case biased in their client's favor. Even though this practice occurs, the cultural value of fair and equal treatment under the law still exists.

9. People experience strong emotional reactions when one's cultural values are violated or when a culture's expected behaviors are ignored.

This is the basis for the strong and oftentimes unexpected emotional response people experience in cross-cultural encounters. People expect specific behaviors in response to their own behavior. When things do not go according to their plan and expectation there is often a strong emotional response. This emotional response can get in the way of their ability to comfortably continue along a certain path.

10. There can be acceptance and rejection of a culture's values at certain times.

It is quite common, for instance, for adolescents in Western societies to challenge authority and go to endless means to create an identity that effectively separates them from the adult members of their society. Such behavior, however, does not preclude them from being considered members of a given culture. It is widely understood that while there may be minor changes with each generation, most will eventually adopt the majority of the mainstream values and practices. One can be a genuine hippie or rapper in his or her youth for instance, and still reenter the mainstream and become a fully-contributing member of society at a later time.

11. **When changes in cultural values are contemplated the reaction that "this will be a difficult uphill battle" is likely.**

   Think back to the definition of culture given in number 1. A general attitude of many civilizations in the past has been the belief that males are dominant over females, and that it should be men who make major decisions, including those that directly affect women. In more recent years, particularly in many nations of the West, this attitude is beginning to change as more and more women begin to influence policy and educational activity. While we are beginning to see change in many nations of the world, albeit slower than many would desire, this shift in thinking is not occurring everywhere.

   This is an interesting example, because it not only shows that different sociocultural groups perceive the world in very different terms, but also that cultural beliefs and attitudes are dynamic and that they can and do change. Many people in the West are now beginning to rethink their attitude and to see the damage they have caused to many in society. This rethinking has taken considerable effort on the part of many special interest groups and activists who have worked endlessly with the hopes of changing people's thinking about gender and society. Many understand the uphill battle that will be fought to change attitudes, behavior, and in some cases laws, but are quite willing to put forth considerable time and effort to push for such measures.

12. **When looking at expected behaviors across cultures, some observations can be summarized in clear contrasts.**

   Such examples as people's use of time, their orientations in space, and deference to youth or aged all provide clear instances of divergent practices. These will become the basis of some exercises in this handbook.

Activity: Aspects of my Own Cultural Upbringing

Instructions

First, individually identify examples from your own past that reflect *each* of the 12 aspects of culture outlined above. Then, share your responses in small groups. Be ready to share an example of each aspect with the larger group.

1. **Culture refers to the human-made part of the environment.**

   My example:

   _____

   _____

   _____

   _____

2. **Culture concerns itself with people's assumptions about life.**

   My example:

   _____

   _____

   _____

   _____

3. **Culture is a collective creation.**

   My example:

   _____

   _____

   _____

   _____

4. **There exist clear childhood experiences that individuals can identify that help to develop and teach particular values and practices.**

   My example:

   _____

   _____

   _____

   _____

5. **Aspects of one's culture that guide his or her behavior are not frequently spoken about.**

   My example:

   _____

   _____

   _____

   _____

6. **As a result of there being a lack of common vocabulary with a common meaning and understanding, people are often unable to discuss culture with others. Cultural differences become most evident in well-meaning clashes.**

   My example:

   _____

   _____

   _____

   _____

7. **Culture allows people to fill in the blanks.**

   My example:

   _____

   _____

   _____

   _____

8. **Cultural values tend to remain in practice, even in spite of compromises or slip-ups.**

   My example:

   _____

   _____

   _____

   _____

9. **People experience strong emotional reactions when one's cultural values are violated or when a culture's expected behaviors are ignored.**
   My example:

   _____

   _____

   _____

   _____

10. **There can be acceptance and rejection of a culture's values at certain times.**
    My example:

    _____

    _____

    _____

    _____

11. **When changes in cultural values are contemplated the reaction that "this will be a difficult uphill battle" is likely.**
    My example:

    _____

    _____

    _____

    _____

12. **When looking at expected behaviors across cultures, some observations can be summarized in clear contrasts.**
    My example:

    _____

    _____

    _____

    _____

Childhood Experiences

Purpose

To identify early socialization experiences that have influenced the cultural values, beliefs and practices held today.

Instructions

In order for culture to be a shared phenomenon it must be effectively transmitted to the young. Generate a list of the expectations of "successful" representatives of American culture. Your list will include desirable beliefs, values, and behaviors.

Beliefs	*Values*	*Behaviors*
_____	_____	_____
_____	_____	_____
_____	_____	_____
_____	_____	_____
_____	_____	_____
_____	_____	_____
_____	_____	_____
_____	_____	_____
_____	_____	_____
_____	_____	_____
_____	_____	_____
_____	_____	_____
_____	_____	_____
_____	_____	_____

Next, what childhood experiences did you have that may have helped you to develop the cultural traits that are expected of you? (For instance, a paper route helps one develop responsibility, individuality, business sense, initiative, and so forth.) Select two entries from each category above and describe early childhood experiences that may have helped you to achieve the desired and expected outcome.

_____

_____

_____

_____

_____

_____

_____

_____

_____

_____

_____

_____

_____

_____

_____

_____

_____

_____

_____

_____

Understanding Cultural Complexity

Purpose

To help you identify the complex and rather broad manner in which people use the concept 'culture.'

Instructions

Review the following material and respond accordingly at each section.

The definition of cultural diversity that is most useful given the time and circumstances in which we live encompasses not only those individuals whose ethnic or cultural heritage originates in another country, but also those among us who have been socialized by different groups; those who may have special educational and other needs (e.g., those who are deaf), those who may share significantly different lifestyles (e.g., rural and urban children, people who live in extreme poverty, drug dependents), those whose identity is critically influenced by their gender, and those who are significantly influenced by variations in class and religion. By this definition, everyone in a pluralistic society such as the United States, Canada, Australia, New Zealand, Great Britain, Israel, and so on can be considered, to some degree, multicultural.

Cushner, McClelland, and Safford (2003) use the Deaf population as an example of a group that has developed a unique culture with both subjective (invisible) and objective (observable) elements. People often think of deaf persons as being just like persons who can hear, except that they sign instead of speak. In most situations, this is not the case; the Deaf community has a culture specific to its members. Speech, for instance, is not valued, and is often considered inappropriate. Most people who are deaf do not sign standard English (e.g., put signs together in standard English word order) except when signing with hearing people. When interacting with other deaf people, American Sign Language or ASL (which has its own syntax) is used.

Accompanying the use of a distinct language among the Deaf population are patterns of behavior that are particular to the group, including some early childhood socialization practices. Children of deaf parents may grow up in environments with much greater visual orientation—lights may accompany a ringing telephone or doorbell, or people may depend upon gestures in interpersonal communication. The Deaf community is also very tightly-knit, placing strong emphasis on social and family ties. Eighty to ninety percent of people who are hearing-impaired marry others with hearing losses. Thus, a strong ingroup orientation develops, making it difficult for outsiders who do not know ASL to enter.

Interactions between hearing and Deaf populations are often filled with feelings of anxiety, uncertainty, and a threat of loss. These feelings are all similar to those encountered in intercultural exchanges. Using this as an example, it is easy to see the range of possible intercultural interactions that can occur between individuals and groups that have distinct subjective cultures.

The field of cross-cultural psychology offers educators the following set of ideas or principles that can be used to study the complexity of culture in schools and communities as well as in the classroom (Pedersen, 2000).

1. **People tend to communicate their cultural identity to others in the broadest possible terms.**

    For instance, upon meeting someone for the first time you may communicate many different things about yourself; including your age, nationality, ethnic group, religious affiliation, where you grew up, and the nature of your family. At other times you may describe your status at work or in the community, your health, your social class, or the way you have come to understand your gender. In other words, people often share such things as demographic information, ethnographic information, as well as information about their status and various affiliations. Each of these sources of cultural identity carries with it associated rules for behavior. We offer such information to new acquaintances because by doing so we give them cultural clues regarding what to expect from us and how to interact with us.

    People, thus, have multiple "cultures" influencing them at various times: their nationality, ethnicity, religion, and gender to name just a few. Each and every one of us may thus be considered multicultural. It might be helpful for people to consider themselves to be comprised of hundreds of different cultural influences.

    What are some of the significant forces in your life that you can identify at this time? Try to identify *at least* five different cultural influences that guide your behavior and thinking. Then tell how each influences you.

Cultural Influence	How it Guides Me
_____	_____
_____	_____
_____	_____
_____	_____
_____	_____
_____	_____

2. **Culture is not static, in the individual nor in the group. One's cultural identity is dynamic and always changing.**

As our environmental circumstances and group associations change, we adapt our cultural identity and behavior pattern accordingly. In certain circumstances our gender-related knowledge and beliefs may be predominant; at another time our religious beliefs may be most evident; and at still other times our ethnicity may be at the forefront. Thus, our own multicultural nature leads to behavior variations that are sometimes difficult to understand and appreciate. It may be more difficult to identify which of the hundreds of cultures are dominant in another person's behavior than it is of our own.

Try to identify *at least* three different occasions when distinctly different cultural forces influence your thoughts and/or actions.

_____

_____

_____

_____

_____

_____

_____

_____

_____

_____

3. **Culture is complex, but it is not chaotic. Good students of culture look for the patterns in people's behavior. Then, once these patterns are understood, the complexity that was perceived at first can be better understood.**

Culture helps individuals make sense of their world and, thereby, to develop more routine in their behavior to fit different environments. Common phrases such as the "culture of the organization," "the culture of the community," or the "culture of the society" refer to the fact that culture is not simply patterned for an individual, but also for a setting, a community, or a society as a whole. When viewed from the outside, these patterns at first can appear quite complicated and difficult to understand. Yet each of us moves quite easily among the cultural patterns with which we are familiar. When confronted by someone whose behavior is *not* familiar, it is the responsibility of the outsider to listen, to observe, and to inquire closely enough so that the patterns of that person (or social group, or society) become evident and understood. To do so decreases the possibility of misunderstanding and conflict, and increases the possibility of new and useful understanding and appreciation.

Try and identify three contexts in which you are familiar that have different patterns of expectations and behavior. In what ways do these patterns differ from other similar contexts in which you are familiar (for instance, you may be aware that the Jewish celebration for the New Year is different from the Christian celebration). Briefly describe these contexts to the best of your ability.

Example 1

_____

_____

_____

_____

_____

_____

_____

Example 2

_____

_____

_____

_____

_____

_____

_____

_____

_____

_____

Example 3

_____

_____

_____

_____

_____

_____

_____

_____

_____

_____

4. Interactions with other cultures can be viewed as a resource for learning.

Culturally-different encounters help to prepare individuals to deal more effectively with the complexity that is increasingly a part of our lives. That, in essence, is one of the major goals of an education that is multicultural — for people to become more complex thinkers, bring more insights into various situations, and thus be more accurate in their interpretations of others' behavior. In short, the number of cultural variables we learn to accommodate will determine our ability to navigate within a fast-moving, ever-changing society.

Tell of an occasion where you interacted with someone from another culture. What do you think you learned about that group as a result of your interaction? How certain are you that your knowledge is accurate?

Interaction

_____

_____

_____

_____

What I Learned

_____

_____

_____

_____

_____

_____

Is my knowledge accurate?

_____

_____

_____

_____

5. Behavior should be judged in relation to its context.

This means that observable behavior cannot be understood apart from the context in which it occurs. Seen outside its context, another's "different" behavior can, at best, seem meaningless, and, at worst, be profoundly misinterpreted. Contextual inquiry allows us to be accurate in our judgments of others.

Consider this example of a particularly troublesome 11-year-old boy who would become rowdy and disruptive in the classroom every day about 2:00 in the afternoon. Inevitably, the teacher sent the child to the office where, because it was late in the day, he was promptly sent home. Defined in terms of the middle-class cultural context of the school, this was definitely a troubled child, and he was so labeled by nearly all the adults in the building. Eventually, an astute counselor recognized a pattern and did some inquiry. It turned out that the mother's boyfriend came home every day about 2:45, oftentimes quite drunk and abusive. In his rage, the boyfriend frequently abused the mother. The boy, quite accurately understanding the cultural patterns of the school and the home, figured out that his misbehavior would result in his being sent home, and that if he was sent home by 2:30, he would arrive before the boyfriend and thus be able to protect his mother. Suddenly our so-called troubled boy's behavior makes sense and he becomes something of a hero because he found a way to protect his vulnerable mother. Again, without full knowledge of the context, behavior is often meaningless or badly misinterpreted.

Give an example of an instance where you initially misunderstood something that was going on. How did you come to finally understand that the situation was different than how it initially appeared?

_____

_____

_____

_____

_____

_____

_____

6. **Person's holding a multicultural perspective continually strive to find common ground between individuals.**

In a sense, we must strive to be cross-eyed. That is, we must be able to see the similarities among people as well as their differences. While it is the differences that tend to stand out and separate people, it is precisely in our similarities where common ground, or a common meeting point, can be found. A multicultural perspective allows two people to disagree without either being wrong. In other words, dialogue between people can continue, which is a key to furthering cross-cultural understanding and mediating differences between people. In this view, cultural differences become tolerable and a "we-they" or an "us-them" debate is avoided. There are no winners and losers. We are all in this together. Either we all win; or we all lose.

Give an example of a compromise you are aware of. What common ground was found between the two parties? How was the common ground established?

_____

_____

_____

_____

_____

_____

_____

_____

_____

_____

_____

_____

_____

_____

_____

_____

Proverbs as a Window into One's Culture

Purpose

1. To examine proverbs as a reflection of culture.

2. To explore the influence of American mainstream values on behavior and educational practice;

3. To compare mainstream values with those of other groups

Instructions

Generating a list of proverbs you have grown up with is an excellent way to explore underlying values that may guide your own behavior. This proverbs exercise has three components:

1. Generate a list of proverbs that you recall hearing as you grew up or that influence you today.
2. Identify what underlying value is expressed by the proverb?
3. State how this value or belief might influence your beliefs and behavior as a teacher?

For instance, for some, the proverb "The early bird catches the worm" may reflect an underlying value of initiative. A person holding this value might be eager to take advantage of the educational opportunities provided to him or her. It may, thus, be easier to teach children who comes to school espousing this value. Or, the proverb, "Children should be seen and not heard" expresses the value of obedience to elders. Such a value might result in a teacher who discourages children from inquiring and asking questions.

On the next pages, either individually or in small groups, try to find *at least* four proverbs to which you can complete all three parts.

Proverb

_____

_____

_____

Underlying Value

_____

_____

_____

Influence on Education

_____

_____

_____

Proverb

_____

_____

_____

Underlying Value

_____

_____

_____

Influence on Education

_____

_____

_____

Proverb

_____

_____

_____

Underlying Value

_____

_____

_____

Influence on Education

_____

_____

_____

Proverb

_____

_____

_____

Underlying Value

_____

_____

_____

Influence on Education

_____

_____

_____

Proverbs: A Cross-Cultural Survey

Following are examples of proverbs from other cultures. For as many as you can, identify an underlying value expressed by each proverb. If possible, give a similar proverb from your cultural tradition.

African

He who sows nettles does not reap roses.

A horse that arrives early gets good drinking water.

By trying often, the monkey learns to jump from the tree.

Little by little grow the bananas.

It takes a village to raise a child.

African American

You got eyes to see and wisdom not to see.

Muddy roads call the milepost a liar.

Every bell ain't a dinner bell.

The graveyard is the cheapest boarding house.

Arabic

An empty drum makes a big sound.

If you take off clothes you are naked. If you take away family, you are nothing.

Doing things quickly is from the devil.

If you want to know somebody, look at her or his friends.

Do not stand in a place of danger trusting in miracles.

Live together like brothers and do business like strangers.

Canadian

Don't sell the bearskin before you kill the bear.

Chinese

Ice three feet thick isn't frozen in a day.

If one plants melons, one gets melons.

The plan of the year is in the spring. The plan of the day is in the morning. The plan of life is in hardship.

Be not afraid of growing slowly, be afraid only of standing still.

Talk doesn't cook rice.

German

Joy, moderation, and rest shut out the doctors.
Young gambler, old beggar.

Indian

I grumbled that I had no shoes until I saw a man who had no feet.
With every rising of the sun think of your life as just begun.
Call on God, but row away from the rocks.

Israeli

Keep a small head.
If you're clever, keep silent.
Life is not a picnic.
Light is not recognized except through darkness.
Don't spit into the well – you might drink from it later.
God could not be everywhere and therefore he made mothers.
A half-truth is a whole lie.
Don't be too sweet lest you be eaten up; don't be too bitter lest you be spewed out.

Italian

He who knows little quickly tells it.
Once the game is over, the king and the pawn go back in the same box.
He who knows nothing doubts nothing.

Japanese

You will gain three moons if you wake early in the morning.
Even monkeys fall from trees.
You can't get clams from a field.
Too many skippers bring the boat to the mountain.
Fall seven times, stand up eight.
Fast Ripe, Fast Rotten.
The reverse side also has a reverse side.

Mexican

To win a dispute is to gain a chicken and lose a cow.
True friendship is one soul shared by two bodies.
Of doctor and poet, musician and madman, we each have a trace.
The sun is the blanket of the poor.

Native American

After dark all cats are leopards. (Zuni)
Do not wrong or hate your neighbor for it is not he that you wrong but
    yourself. (Pima)
Every animal knows more than you do. (Nez Perce)
It is less of a problem to be poor than to be dishonest. (Anishinabe)
A rocky vineyard does not need a prayer, but a pick ax. (Navajo)
We will be known forever by the tracks we leave. (Dakota)
Those that lie down with dogs, get up with fleas. (Blackfoot)

Polish

Fish, to taste good, must swim three times: in water, in butter, and in wine.
The greater love is a mother's; then comes a dog's; then a sweetheart's.
Do not push the river, it will flow by itself.
A good painter need not give a name to his picture, a bad one must.
Even a clock that does not work is right twice a day.
A guest sees more in an hour than the host in a year.

Russian

Every peasant is proud of the pond in his village because from it he meas-
    ures the sea.
Every road has two directions.
The hammer shatters glass but forges steel.
He who doesn't risk never gets to drink champagne.
Ask a lot, but take what is offered.

Spanish

One bird in the hand is worth one thousand flying.
Your getting up early doesn't make the sun rise earlier.
Don't speak unless you can improve on the silence.
From a fallen tree, all make kindling.
If your house is on fire, warm yourself by it.

Cultural Values in American Society

Purpose

To explore the relationship between cultural values and their expression in institutions, especially the American school, and to consider how some of these values may be changing.

Instructions

Read the following discussion of traditional American values. Then, respond to the questions according to how you see the particular value expressed in society.

American culture is complex, and many would say that it is difficult to identify a national culture or what might be called "typical" American cultural patterns. Many European Americans, for instance, think of themselves as having no culture, as being citizens of a nation too young to have really developed a culture. Nothing, however, could be further from the truth. Every group of people with any history has created a culture that pervades their thoughts and actions. American society is rich with diverse cultural patterns that, for many, come together in the schools. Since cultural patterns associated with the European American middle class have provided the foundation in most schools in this society, these patterns will be analyzed in terms of the school experience and school readiness. You should be making comparisons to other groups within American society.

A brief reflection on American history suggests that those who colonized North America had relatively weak ties to their homelands. The extended family, important in the country of origin, was separated, leaving the nuclear family as the predominant source of strength and identity. This had a tremendous influence on the development of the "American" character, since people's orientation had to shift from the larger collective to the individual or nuclear family unit. It is here that we see the beginnings of an individualistic orientation. In addition, as people came to settle the United States, the need to adjust to uncertainty, as well as to focus on change and development for survival, become paramount. Many of these values are in conflict with those held in many ethnic communities today.

Over the years, a dominant European-American middle-class culture has emerged that rests on six major values (Samover, Porter and Jain, 1981). In the previous exercise you explored values by looking at proverbs and sayings that have become a part of our folk wisdom. Since such proverbs express the values of a people, they are an excellent indicator of the folk-knowledge that supports and integrates society.

Reflect upon each mainstream value presented below and how it has influenced schools. Then, try to identify where another group's cultural value might be in support or conflict with it.

---

1. **European-Americans have a tendency to view themselves as separate from nature and able to master or control their environment.**

   As a result, a high value is placed on science and technology as the predominant means of interacting with the world. This results in objectivity, rationality, materialism, and a need for concrete evidence. Proverbs and sayings such as "Necessity is the mother of invention," and "We'll cross that bridge when we come to it" reflect this belief.

How do you see this value expressed in society?

_____

_____

_____

How do you see this value expressed in schools?

_____

_____

_____

Can you think of any other proverbs or sayings that reflect a similar sentiment?

_____

_____

_____

Can you identify a cultural group whose values might support or be in conflict with this one? Support your response.

_____

_____

_____

Do you have any indication that this value is undergoing change in recent years?
    If so, please explain.

_____

_____

_____

---

2. European-Americans are action-oriented.
    As with number 1, this results in measurable accomplishments and an emphasis on efficiency and practicality. Progress and change thus become important concepts. Our schools expect such an orientation, as evidenced by an emphasis on testing and measurement as well as a nearly religious belief in the efficiency of paperwork assignments. Proverbs such as "Seeing is believing," and "The proof is in the pudding" emphasize this cultural trait.

How do you see this value expressed in society?

_____

_____

_____

How do you see this value expressed in schools?

_____

_____

_____

Can you think of any other proverbs or sayings that reflect a similar sentiment?

_____

_____

_____

Can you identify a cultural group whose values might support or be in conflict with this one? Support your response.

_____

_____

_____

Do you have any indication that this value is undergoing change in recent years?
    If so, please explain.

_____

_____

_____

> **3. European-Americans have a future orientation; they believe in the promise that things will be bigger and better.**
>
>   Most middle-class European-Americans are seldom content with the present; they wish not to be considered old-fashioned, and they believe that effort applied in the present will affect their future. Progress is, in many ways, their most important product. Proverbs such as "I think I can, I think I can," "A penny saved is a penny earned," "From little acorns, mighty oaks grow," and even the more recent "No pain—no gain" reflect this tendency.

How do you see this value expressed in society?

_____

_____

_____

How do you see this value expressed in schools?

_____

_____

_____

Can you think of any other proverbs or sayings that reflect a similar sentiment?

_____

_____

_____

Can you identify a cultural group whose values might support or be in conflict with this one? Support your response.

_____

_____

_____

Do you have any indication that this value is undergoing change in recent years?

If so, please explain.

_____

_____

_____

---

4. European-Americans are self-motivated and are comfortable setting their own goals and directions.

From an early age, the majority of European-Americans are encouraged to reach out on their own, to attempt for themselves, to satisfy their own needs. Such proverbs as "Nothing ventured, nothing gained," "If at first you don't succeed, try, try again," and "The early bird catches the worm" reflect this trait.

How do you see this value expressed in society?

_____

_____

_____

How do you see this value expressed in schools?

_____

_____

_____

Can you think of any other proverbs or sayings that reflect a similar sentiment?

_____

_____

_____

Can you identify a cultural group whose values might support or be in conflict with this one? Support your response.

_____

_____

_____

Do you have any indication that this value is undergoing change in recent years?

   If so, please explain.

_____

_____

_____

---

5. European-Americans have a strong sense of individuality.

   The belief that the "self" is an individual that is separate from others results in a tendency to emphasize individual initiative, independence, action, and interests. Many believe that to be an effective person, one must be responsible, independent, and have an internal locus of control and set of standards. One should not depend on others for identity. European-American culture, thus, expects and encourages independence, even within the larger group. From an early age, children are encouraged to make their own decisions and to develop their individual skills and abilities. In the traditional school, children are expected to work alone in their seats, rarely coming together for group work. How many of you have heard teachers say, "Keep your eyes on your own paper," or "Don't talk with your neighbors"? A cursory review of most grade school report cards gives evidence of the emphasis on this trait. Consider such statements as "Johnny is able to work independently," "Mary works well on her own," or "Sean is a responsible student." Proverbs such as "Too many cooks spoil the broth," "Don't judge a book by its cover," and "God helps those who help themselves" stress this value.

How do you see this value expressed in society?

_____

_____

_____

How do you see this value expressed in schools?

_____

_____

_____

Can you think of any other proverbs or sayings that reflect a similar sentiment?

_____

_____

_____

Can you identify a cultural group whose values might support or be in conflict with this one? Support your response.

_____

_____

_____

Do you have any indication that this value is undergoing change in recent years?

If so, please explain.

_____

_____

_____

---

6. **Finally, European-Americans believe in the mutability of human nature.**

That is, they subscribe to the notion that it is relatively easy to change and that their cultural environment can mold people. This belief underlies the assimilationist ideology that has pervaded American public education for so many years. "A stranger is only a friend you haven't met yet," and "Leaders are made, not born" may reflect this notion.

How do you see this value expressed in society?

_____

_____

_____

How do you see this value expressed in schools?

_____

_____

_____

Can you think of any other proverbs or sayings that reflect a similar sentiment?

_____

_____

_____

Can you identify a cultural group whose values might support or be in conflict with this one? Support your response.

_____

_____

_____

Do you have any indication that this value is undergoing change in recent years?
    If so, please explain.

_____

_____

_____

Family Tree: Tracing One's Roots and Family Experiences

Purpose

To discover your family's experiences in past generations and compare it to immigrants and refugees today.

Instructions

Respond to the reflective questions below.

Most of us can trace our family history, or roots, to someplace. Speak with family members and look through old family photographs (if you have any) to trace your family's heritage as far back as possible. *If you are adopted or do not know your ancestors, respond in terms of an adoptive or foster family, or one to which you closely identify.* Respond to the following questions as best you can and share your responses with others.

From what parts of the world did your family (or families) originate?

_____

_____

_____

What motivated your ancestors to leave their homeland for a new world? When did they leave? If your ancestors were always in North America, what was their life like prior to European contact?

_____

_____

_____

What hardships did your ancestors face in previous generations, either when they first arrived or soon after contact? What did they do to overcome any hardships? Do they recall any prejudice that was experienced?

_____

_____

_____

What did your ancestors do in the previous 2-3 generations? How did this influence what the family does today?

_____

_____

_____

_____

_____

_____

What languages did your ancestors speak? What has happened to these languages in your family today?

_____

_____

_____

_____

_____

_____

What family traditions or practices have been carried out over the years that are special or unique to your family?

_____

_____

_____

_____

_____

What do you know of the meaning behind your family name? What does it mean? How, if at all, has it changed over the years? Do you know the reason for any changes?

_____

_____

_____

_____

_____

How are the experiences of your family similar to, or different from, those faced by various immigrants or refugees today?

_____

_____

_____

_____

_____

In what ways was this an easy or difficult exercise for you to do? Under what circumstances might an exercise like this be difficult for a student to do? What might you do to modify it in special circumstances?

_____

_____

_____

_____

_____

Who Am I?

Purpose

To generate a list reflecting the categories to which you identify.

Instructions

Complete the statement, "I am a(n) ___," 20 times in the spaces provided below rather quickly. Do not think too long about your responses as no answers are right or wrong.

1. I am a(n) _____.
2. I am a(n) _____.
3. I am a(n) _____.
4. I am a(n) _____.
5. I am a(n) _____.
6. I am a(n) _____.
7. I am a(n) _____.
8. I am a(n) _____.
9. I am a(n) _____.
10. I am a(n) _____.
11. I am a(n) _____.
12. I am a(n) _____.
13. I am a(n) _____.
14. I am a(n) _____.
15. I am a(n) _____.
16. I am a(n) _____.
17. I am a(n) _____.
18. I am a(n) _____.
19. I am a(n) _____.
20. I am a(n) _____.

When you have finished, divide your responses according to the underlying categories you are able to recognize. This strategy can help you gain a picture of the image you have of yourself.

How many entries represent individual
traits (singer, dancer, student, for instance)?   _____

How many entries represent collective
affiliations (member of the choir or dance
company, for instance)?   _____

Ethnic group identification is often used to describe human groups who share a common historical heritage and a sense of peoplehood, or the feeling that one's own destiny is somehow linked with that of others.

How early on your list did ethnic identity appear?   _____

What does its placement suggest about you and your identity with an ethnic group? If it appeared toward the bottom of the list, to what do you attribute this? If it appeared toward the top of the list, to what do you attribute this? If it did not appear at all, to what do you attribute this?

_____

_____

_____

_____

What would you miss if your ethnicity was taken away from you?

_____

_____

_____

_____

Compare your responses with others. Discuss the relative number of individualistic versus collective references on your list. How does the placement of your ethnic-group identity relate to the number of individualistic or collective identifications on your list? What might this mean about the importance of ethnicity to some people?

_____

_____

_____

_____

_____

_____

_____

_____

_____

_____

_____

_____

_____

_____

_____

_____

_____

_____

_____

The Culture Learning Process

The following is further expanded upon in Human Diversity in Education: An Integrative Approach, *4th ed., 2003 Kenneth Cushner, Averil McClelland and Philip Safford*

Purpose

To identify the results of major socializing influences on your life.

Instructions

As suggested earlier, individuals tend to identify themselves in a broad manner and in terms of many physical and social attributes. For example, a young man might identify himself as an attractive, athletic, Asian-American who intends to be a doctor and live in upper-class society. It is important to note also that others also identify individuals according to these attributes and that interactions among individuals are often shaped by such identifications. Incorporated into Figure 11-1 are twelve such attributes or manifestations of culture that researchers suggest influence teaching and learning. Who learns what, how, and when it is learned will be briefly described below. You will be asked to examine yourself along each of these attributes.

What is Learned: The Attributes of Culture

Race: Biologically speaking, race refers to the clustering of inherited physical characteristics that favor adaptation to a particular ecological area. However, race is culturally defined in the sense that different societies emphasize different sets of physical characteristics when referring to the same race. In fact, the term is so imprecise that it has even been used to refer to a wide variety of categories that are not physical, e.g., linguistic categories (the *English-speaking race*), religious categories (the *Jewish* race), national categories (the *Italian* race), and even to somewhat mythological categories (the *Teutonic* race). Although race has often been defined as a biological category, it has been argued that race as a biological concept is of little use because there are no "pure" races. Recent research in mapping the genetic code of five people of different races demonstrates that the concept of race has no scientific basis (*Akron Beacon Journal, 2000*). In the United States, race is judged largely on the basis of skin color, which some people consider very meaningful and use as a criterion for extending or withholding privileges of

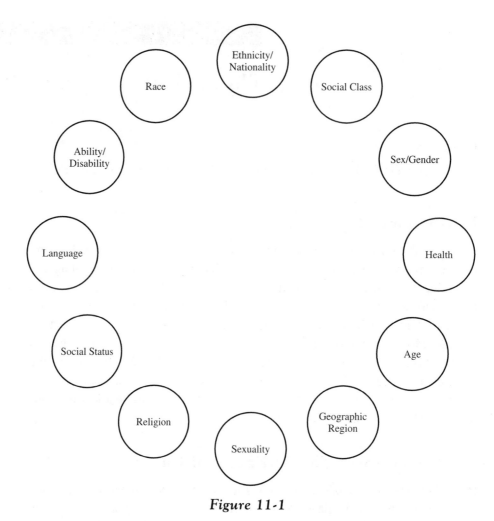

Figure 11-1

various kinds. Racism results from the transformation of race prejudice and/or ethnocentrism through the exercise of power against a racial group defined as inferior, by individuals or institutions, with the intentional or unintentional support of an entire culture. Simply stated, preference for or belief in the superiority of one own racial group might be called racism.

How is race evident in your life?

_____

_____

_____

Sex/Gender: Sex is culturally defined on the basis of a particular set of physical characteristics. In this case, however, the characteristics are related to male and female reproduction. Cultural meanings associated with gender are expressed in terms of socially valued behaviors (e.g., nurturing the young and providing food) which are assigned according to sex. Such culturally assigned behaviors eventually become so accepted that they come to be thought of as natural for that sex. Thus, gender is what it *means* to be male or female in a society, and gender roles are those sets of behaviors thought by a particular people to be "normal" and "good" when carried out by the assigned sex.

How is sex/gender evident in your life?

_____

_____

_____

Health: Health is culturally defined according to a particular group's view of what physical, mental, and emotional states constitute a "healthy" person. The "expert" opinion of the medical profession usually guides a society's view of health. Although a medical model has dominated cultural definitions of health in Western societies, most disabilities (mental retardation, deafness, blindness, etc.) are not judged in terms of this model's norms. Thus it is possible to be a healthy blind or retarded person. Nor would a person with cerebral palsy be considered "sick."

In the United States and most of the industrialized world, the prevailing health system is almost totally biomedical. However, alternative systems such as acupuncture, holistic medicine, and faith healing are available, and the acceptance of alternative systems varies widely both within and between social groups.

How is health evident in your life?

_____

_____

_____

Ability/Disability: As with definitions of health, ability and disability are culturally defined according to society's view about what it means to be physically, emotionally, and mentally "able." The categories of "ability" and "disability" refer to a wide variety of mental and physical characteristics: intelligence, emotional stability, impairment of sensory and neural systems, and impairment of movement. The social significance of these characteristics may vary by setting as well. For example, the terms "learning disability" or "learning disabled" are terms primarily used with reference to schooling and are rarely used outside of school. Indeed, it may be that the current emphasis on learning disability in American schools is primarily a reflection of a technologically complex society's concern about literacy.

How is ability/disability evident in your life?

_____

_____

_____

_____

Social Class: Social class is culturally defined on the basis of those criteria on which a person or social group may be ranked in relation to others in a stratified (or layered) society. There is considerable debate about the criteria that determine social class. Some identify class membership primarily in terms of wealth and its origin (inherited or newly-earned). Other commonly used criteria include the amount of one's education, power, and influence.

How is social class evident in your life?

_____

_____

_____

_____

Ethnicity/Nationality: Ethnicity is culturally defined according to the knowledge, beliefs and behavior patterns shared by a group of people with the same history and the same language. Ethnicity carries a strong sense of "peoplehood," that is, of loyalty to a "community of memory" (Bellah, Madsen, Sullivan, Swindler, and Tipton, 1985). It is also related to the ecological niche in which an ethnic group has found itself and to adaptations people make to those environmental conditions.

The category of nationality is culturally defined on the basis of shared citizenship that may or may not include a shared ethnicity. In the contemporary world, the population of most nations includes citizens (and resident noncitizens) who vary in ethnicity. While we are accustomed to this idea in the United States, we are sometimes unaware that it is also the case in other nations. Thus, we tend to identify all people from Japan as Japanese, all people from France as French, and so forth. Similarly, when American citizens of varying ethnic identities go abroad, they tend to be identified as "Americans." Being Chinese-American, for instance, may mean little outside the borders of the United States.

How are the concepts of ethnicity and nationality evident in your life?

_____

_____

_____

_____

Religion/Spirituality: Religion and spirituality are culturally defined on the basis of a shared set of ideas about the relationship of the earth and the people on it to a deity or deities and a shared set of rules for living moral values that will enhance that relationship. A set of behaviors identified with worship is also commonly shared. Religious identity may include membership in a worldwide-organized religion (e.g., Islam, Christianity, Judaism, Buddhism, Taoism), or in smaller (but also worldwide) sects belonging to each of the larger religions (e.g., Catholic or Protestant Christianity or Conservative, Reformed, or Hasidic Judaism). Religious identity may also include a large variety of spiritualistic religions, sometimes called pagan or Goddess religions. These are often but not always associated with indigenous peoples in the Americas and other parts of the world.

How is religion and/or spirituality evident in your life?

_____

_____

_____

_____

Geographic Location: Geographic location is culturally defined by the characteristics (topographical features, natural resources) of the ecological environment in which one lives. This may include the characteristics of one's neighborhood or community (rural, suburban, urban), and/or the natural and climatic features of one's region (mountainous, desert, plains, coastal, hot, cold, wet, dry). It has been argued that, in the United States, one's regional identity functions in the same way as one's national heritage (Yetman, 1991). Thus, southerners, westerners, and Midwesterners are identified and often identify themselves as members of ethnic-like groups, with the same kinds of loyalties, sense of community, and language traits.

How is geographic or regional identity evident in your life?

_____

_____

_____

_____

Age: Age is culturally defined according to the length of time one has lived and the state of physical and mental development one has attained. Chronological age is measured in different ways by different social groups or societies. Some calculate it in calendar years, others by natural cycles such as phases of the moon, and still others by the marking of major natural or social events. Most humans view such development as a matter of "stages," but the nature and particular characteristics of each "stage" may differ widely. In most western societies, for example, age cohort groups are usually identified as infancy, childhood, adolescence, adulthood, and old age. "Normal" development markers include the acquisition of motor and language skills (infancy and childhood), the ability to understand and use abstract concepts (childhood and adolescence), and the ability to assume responsibility for oneself and others (adolescence and adulthood). In other societies, these cohort groups may differ. For example, in many nonwestern societies, the cohort group we define as adolescents may not exist at all, and the classifications of childhood and old age may be longer or shorter. Also, different societies place different value on age, some placing more emphasis on youth while others venerate the aged.

How is age evident in your life?

_____

_____

_____

_____

Sexuality: Sexuality is culturally defined on the basis of particular patterns of sexual self-identification, behavior, and interpersonal relationships (Herek, 1986). There is growing evidence that one's sexual orientation is, in part, a function of one's innate biological characteristics (LeVay and Hunter, 1994). Culturally speaking, sexuality is tied to a number of factors: sexual behavior, gender identity (both internal and external), affiliation, and role behavior. Like health, sexuality has a variety of orientations. Because sexuality is frequently linked to one's deepest, most meaningful experiences (both religious and interpersonal), people who deviate from socially approved norms are often socially ostracized and sometimes physically abused or even killed. This is currently the case with homosexuality in the United States, where the prevailing view of sexuality is bimodal; only male and female are identified as possibilities. In other societies, additional possibilities are available. The Lakota Sioux, for example, approve four sexual orientations: biological males who possess largely masculine traits, biological males who possess largely feminine traits, biological females who possess largely feminine traits, and biological females who possess largely masculine traits. The role of the female-identified male in Lakota society is called berdache, and is accorded high honor as possessing multiple traits and characteristics. Berdache tend to be teachers and artists, and if a berdache takes an interest in one's child or children, it is considered to be an advantage.

How is sexuality evident in your life?

_____

_____

_____

_____

Language: The cultural definition of language is "a shared system of vocal sounds and/or nonverbal behaviors by which members of a group communicate with one another" (Gollnick and Chinn, 1990). Language may be the most significant source of cultural learning because it is through language that most other cultural knowledge is acquired. Considerable research on the relation of brain function to language gives evidence that human beings are "hard wired" for language development at a particular stage in brain development (Chomsky, 1966). That is, children who are in the company of other people appear to be "programmed" to learn whatever spoken language or sign system is used around them. Children even invent their own language systems, complete with syntactical structures, if no other language is available. It may also be that this "program" decreases in power (or disappears altogether) at a certain point, helping to explain why it is more difficult for older children and adults to acquire a new language. Language is meaningful in terms of both its verbal properties (what we "name" things, people, ideas), and in terms of its nonverbal properties (its norms regarding interpersonal distance, meaningful gestures, and so forth).

How is language evident in your life?

_____

_____

_____

_____

Social Status: Social status is culturally defined on the basis of the prestige, social esteem, and/or honor accorded an individual or group by other social groups or by society (Berger and Berger, 1972). Social status cuts across the other categories, since every social group or society appears to construct hierarchies of honor, prestige, and value with which to "sort out" its members, often on the basis of such attributes as race, age, gender, ability, religion, and so forth. In some cases, social status varies with social class; in many other cases, however, social class does not explain one's status in a social group or society. Thus, persons may occupy a high place in the class system in terms of income and power but not be accorded prestige or honor. The children of a newly-wealthy family who can well afford to be sent to Harvard, for example, may have little prestige among the sons and daughters of inherited wealth. Similarly, there may be people accorded high status in the society who occupy relatively low-class positions. In U.S. society, many entertainers and sports figures fit this description.

How is social status evident in your life?

_____

_____

_____

_____

While there is some overlap among these twelve attributes of culture, the important point to remember is that a particular society or social group culturally defines each of them. The cultural identity of all individuals (i.e., their knowledge, attitudes, values, and skills) is formed through one's experience with these twelve attributes.

Now, look closely at Figure 2 that details these 12 attributes of culture. Allow these to represent some of the hundreds of cultural influences that impact each individual, including yourself. Take the time to examine your own background in terms of each of these. While before you merely identified how each of these attributes were evident in your life, *here you should examine how your views on the world, your behavior and your values have been influenced by each of these.*

For instance, for geographic location, a student might say she or he is from the State of Washington, which is relatively conservative but quite environmentally responsible. The person might value the wilderness and nature in general, and enjoy being outdoors.

Race:

_____

_____

_____

_____

Sex/gender:

_____

_____

_____

_____

Health:

_____

_____

_____

_____

Ability/disability:

_____

_____

_____

_____

Social Class:

_____

_____

_____

_____

Ethnicity/nationality:

_____

_____

_____

_____

Religion/spirituality:

_____

_____

_____

_____

Geographic location:

_____

_____

_____

_____

_____

Age:

_____

_____

_____

_____

_____

Sexuality:

_____

_____

_____

_____

Language:

_____

_____

_____

_____

_____

Social status:

_____

_____

_____

_____

_____

Which of the attributes holds the most significance for you?

_____

_____

_____

_____

_____

_____

_____

Which of the attributes holds the least significance for you?

_____

_____

_____

_____

_____

How is involvement in the groups that are important to you expressed in your day-to-day life?

_____

_____

_____

_____

_____

Give examples of experiences you have had that have increased or decreased your sense of belonging to a certain group.

_____

_____

_____

_____

_____

Which groups place you at an advantage in American society? How?

_____

_____

_____

_____

_____

_____

_____

Which groups place you at a disadvantage in American society? How?

_____

_____

_____

_____

_____

_____

_____

Share your responses with others in small groups. Were there some aspects that were more difficult to discuss than others? What do you notice about the different responses provided by peers who you would consider to be in a similar group as you? What does this suggest about within group differences?

_____

_____

_____

_____

_____

_____

How Culture Is Learned: The Socializing Agents

Purpose

To gain an understanding of how various dimensions of society mediate and modify what individuals learn in a given culture.

Instructions

Read the following and respond to the reflective questions.

It is important to understand that we acquire the specific knowledge, attitudes, skills, and values that form our cultural identity through a variety of socializing agents. These socializing agents mediate the various attributes of culture and give them a particular "cultural spin." Thus, one's understanding of race, gender, social class, disability, age, sexuality, and so forth depends, in large part, upon the interpretation and transmission by the particular families, schools, peer groups, neighborhoods, workplaces, churches, and communities that one affiliates with at a particular time. Each of these socializing agents has its own slightly different interpretation of a particular cultural attribute that it passes on to its members.

In contemporary social life some socializing agents such as families and peer groups operate face-to-face, while others, such as the mass media, use technology to operate from a distance. Television, VCRs, the Internet and the recording industry, for example, exert significant influence on the self-perceived identity of many young people. Referred to by some as the "third educator" (following family and school), television influences young people's acquisition of basic language and visual and aural skills. It also influences their ideas of "appropriate" dress, language, attitudes and values. These media lessons not only affect young people's "picture" of themselves, but also affects the picture that adults have of them. The media also teaches, for instance, about older people. The visual image of the woman who has "fallen and can't get up" describes older people as weak, helpless, and slightly hysterical.

Other technological tools such as computers and microwave ovens appear to exert significant influence on our notions of time. Teachers and other human service providers have noticed, for example, that over the past 20 years or so both children and adults exhibit a shorter attention span. They seem to have become accustomed to receiving information and accomplishing tasks in shorter periods of time and are unwilling or unable to persevere in tasks that take a long time.

Other socializing agents include the performing and visual arts and, in the United States at least, sports. Each of these carry cultural messages that shape people's attitudes, values, and behavior. The aesthetic value of language, music, dance, and theater as well as ideals of moral and ethical behavior are presented through the arts. Behavioral ideals such as good sportsmanship, personal achievement, and competition are also taught through sport. Other qualities may also be taught through these media; violence, for example, is an increasing part of movies, television, and sports. The contemporary nature of national sports teams as bottom-line businesses comes increasingly into competition with our professed value of "sportsmanlike" competition.

Figure 12-1 provides a visual overview of how the various components or attributes of culture are filtered down to individuals through the many socializing agents they encounter. Although the components of culture (race, language, sexuality, etc.) are universal and appear in all cultures, the socializing agents

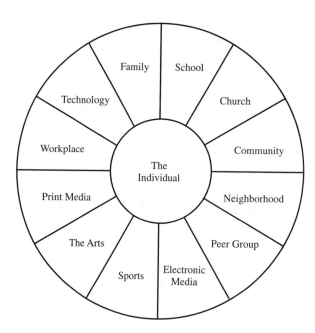

Figure 12-1

(family, schools, media, etc.) that transmit them vary considerably from one culture to another. In most industrialized societies, for example, a wide variety of socializing agents bombard people daily, often with contradictory messages. In agriculturally-oriented societies, on the other hand, a few primary socializing agents (e.g., family, gender, and community group) may share the bulk of the culture filtering process. The result is that individuals in different cultures develop very different worldviews.

Figure 12-2 merges the previous figures and thus provides us with a greater understanding of the multiple influences (the 'hundred' cultures) that are at play in people's lives. By spinning the inner as well as the outer circles

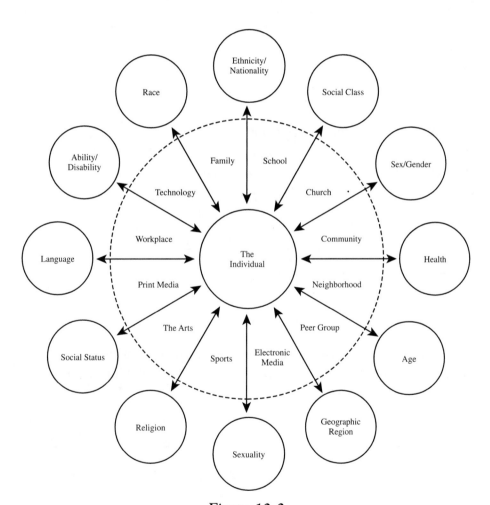

Figure 12-2

one can easily begin to see how different people can acquire different cultural patterns. In the space provided below, explore three possible combinations of cultural attributes and socializing agents from your own experience and upbringing.

One example of the interaction between cultural attribute _____ and socializing agent _____ in my life and its influence on me has been _____

_____

_____

_____

_____

_____

_____

Another example of the interaction between cultural attribute _____ and socializing agent _____ in my life and its influence on me has been _____

_____

_____

_____

_____

_____

_____

A third example of the interaction between cultural attribute _____ and socializing agent _____ in my life and its influence on me has been _____

_____

_____

_____

_____

_____

Getting to Know the Culture of Others: Intercultural Interaction

 Go to www.mhhe.com/cushner4e and click on *Human Diversity in Action* for a listing of Web Links.

Understanding Misunderstanding: Barriers to Dealing with Diversity

*Reprinted with permission.
Social Education, vol.53,
No.5*

Kenneth Cushner and Gregory Trifonovitch

Educators are futurists; they must anticipate tomorrow's needs and equip today's students with the necessary skills to meet those needs. Our nation and world must deal with opportunities and challenges never before encountered. Cities and schools are becoming increasingly integrated, the international business community continues to expand, immigrant and refugee populations swell national borders, and people the world over desire the same limited resources.

As a result, people have increasing contacts with others whose cultural backgrounds, attitudes, hopes and dreams, and ways of doing things differ significantly from their own. We have become so interconnected and interdependent that our planet's survival depends upon the smooth functioning and successful interaction of numerous governments, economies, and technologies.

Increasing interaction increases the likelihood of conflict and confrontation and creates the perception that we face a crisis. The Chinese word for crisis, 'wei-chi', may help us understand this situation. The first part of the word, 'wei', means danger. The latter part, 'chi', means opportunity. Crisis need not present only threat; the situation may present the opportunity to learn and grow.

Successful outcomes between and among people of diversity depend ultimately upon the extent to which positive and functional perspectives and interrelationships of those of different backgrounds emerge. The schools must, therefore, address this challenge on many fronts. It is projected that, by the year 2020, half of the students in our schools will be from an ethnic or national minority group. As professionals, we must interact effectively and teach students from diverse backgrounds to interact with confidence in the interdependent world they are certain to inherit. Beyond the obvious traditional distinctions between cultural and ethnic groups that most people make are the subtle differences that distinguish many subgroups within our schools, communities, and nation. Schools host a range of students: one in four is poverty-stricken (Kennedy, Jung, and Orland 1986); one in seven is a potential dropout (Hodgkinson *1985),* and one in five lives in a single-parent home (Center for Educational Statistics 1987).

This paper attempts to expand the definition of cultural differences to help educators understand some of the difficulties they face when interacting with those from a variety of different backgrounds. This requires addressing intercultural interaction itself as content within the school experience.

Certain barriers or obstacles to achieving an ability to interact effectively with those different from ourselves lie deep in our sociological, historical, and psychological roots. These should all be addressed by teachers and students. Of particular interest are barriers at the individual level that result, in part, because people are the product of a given culture. What we suggest is that obstacles to learning about those who are different from ourselves are a result of being socialized in any given culture. Cross-cultural psychology and its applications to intercultural or cross-cultural training offer some insights into these obstacles, including, but not limited to, defining culture itself, ethnocentrism, the nature of culture learning, the adjustment process, perception and categorization, and ultimately the attribution process. We propose that awareness of these obstacles and how they affect one's ability to learn about others is fundamental to the task of dealing with diversity. Simultaneously, the reader should come away with increased understanding of the concept of culture itself and increased cultural self-awareness.

Defining Culture and Broadening Its Scope

There are hundreds of definitions of the term 'culture'. Gerte Hofstede (1980) describes culture as "mass programming of the mind" and differentiates three levels in a hierarchical form. Cultural universals found among all people form a foundation. At this level are such biological responses as sucking, sneezing, and walking, and such things as people's need for and ability to communicate with others. Next, at the shared-group level, people from a common heritage learn certain things in a similar manner. Using the cultural universal of communication as an example, we find that, in the shared-group level, people learn to speak a certain verbal language while learning to use nonverbal cues in a similar manner. At the top of the hierarchy are individual strengths and interests that might differ from others, yet are still considered acceptable to the group. Some people, for instance are effective oral communicators; others prefer the solitude of writing; some reach out through various art forms. It is the level of the shared group that is of most interest when considering cultural differences.

There is yet another distinction or characteristic of culture that is essential for thinking about interaction and adjustment while working with diversity. That is the distinction between objective and subjective components of culture

(Triandis 1972). Objective components of a culture refer to the visible, tangible aspects of a particular group of people. Aspects such as a people's artifacts, clothing, and foods fall into this category. Most people think of these when considering cultural differences as the most obvious components of a culture to study and analyze. The more potent and powerful aspects of a culture, however, are its subjective components, including the less visible, less tangible aspects that people carry around in their minds. Falling into this category are characteristics such as attitudes, values, norms of behavior, and the roles people assume. Subjective components of culture are much more difficult to study, inspect, and analyze. It is at the level of people's subjective culture that most intercultural misunderstandings and communication problems apparently exist. It is here that the study of intercultural interaction should focus.

By distinguishing objective and subjective components of culture, it becomes possible to expand our perspective on what constitutes a culturally different group relative to one's own. When individuals who have been socialized by groups with different subjective cultural patterns come together, a cross-cultural interaction occurs. With it come all the potential problems and opportunities. It then becomes apparent that cross-cultural interactions occur not only between individuals of distinct national or ethnic heritages, but as well between individuals who interact rather frequently who have been socialized in different ways. A definition of diversity can be expanded to include members of the many special-needs populations (the hearing impaired, the visually impaired, the gifted and talented), the many subcultures in society today (gays, children at risk, drug dependents), gender differences, as well as the distinctions that occur between socioeconomic groups (the under class, lower class, middle class, and upper class). Each of these groups has a distinct subjective culture, including unique value systems, norms of behavior, modes of interaction, socialization practices, linguistic patterns, and so forth.

For instance, we often think of hearing impaired persons as being just like persons who can hear except that they sign instead of speak. In most cases, this is not the case; the Deaf community has a culture specific to its members. Speech is not valued, and is often considered inappropriate. Most people who are deaf do not sign English except when signing with hearing people. When interacting with other deaf people, American Sign Language is used. Accompanying the use of this distinct language are particular patterns of behavior, including early childhood socialization practices. Children of deaf parents grow up in environments with much greater visual orientation; lights may accompany a ringing telephone or doorbell and people grow to depend upon gestures in interpersonal communication. The Deaf community is also tight-knit, placing strong emphasis on social and family ties. Eighty to 90 percent of deaf people marry deaf persons. As with other cultures, a strong in-group orientation develops, making it difficult for outsiders to enter.

Interactions between hearing and hearing-impaired populations are often filled with feelings of anxiety, uncertainty, and a threat of loss. These feelings are all similar to those encountered in cross-cultural encounters. It is easy to see the vast range of prospects that exist for cross-cultural interaction among individuals and groups that share distinct subjective cultures.

Socialization and Ethnocentrism

Socialization is the process by which individuals learn what is required to be successful members of a given group. Socialization is a unique process in that it looks simultaneously to the future and the past; it looks forward to where persons are expected to be and backward to determine what behaviors, attitudes, values, and beliefs (subjective culture) are important to continue.

Socialization is such a potent and powerful process that people are hardly aware that other realities could exist. One consequence of this is that people tend to view the world solely from their own viewpoint and to think their way of doing things the best. Other ways are seen as second-rate, at best. This result, referred to as ethnocentrism, suggests that people have the tendency to view the world from their own perspective. Although a degree of ethnocentrism is necessary for binding a group of people together, it may become an obstacle when it becomes necessary to interact and work with others, especially if people believe their own way the best. A reasonable goal in cross-cultural training or intercultural education is to help others develop an ethnorelative perspective; that is, the ability to understand that there are other equally valid ways of viewing the world. In addition, we must help people learn how to accept ethnocentrism as a fact about themselves as well as others.

One's Culture Is a Secret

Another problem in learning about culture and the difficulties encountered in cross-cultural interaction is that people have little knowledge about themselves. One's own culture, like one's own language, is a secret. One way of looking at culture is to consider it as a set of hidden, recurring patterns of behavior and thought; hidden because each person learns to behave appropriately in a given culture. It thus becomes difficult to explain why persons do what they do and how they learned those behaviors.

The learning of language provides an example. How could one teach someone learning to speak English to pronounce this sentence correctly, *Can you tell me the* time? when one might more easily say, *Can you dell me the dime? What* might persons be told to enable them to make the appropriate sounds?

If you have determined that a little puff of air passes out of the mouth when the 't' sound is made in such words as 'tell' and 'time' as opposed to the 'd' sound, you are on track to discovering the technique. English speakers tend to aspirate stops; that is, some air passes out of the mouth when such letters as 't', 'p', and 'k' are spoken. A further fact must also be learned: stops are aspirated at the beginning of words but not at the end. We don't aspirate the 't' in 'hit', 'bit', or 'cat'. How were these rules learned? Probably not by sitting down and studying language texts or by being taught by parents, but by trial and error in the early years having proper models and consistent reinforcement. This pattern is often hidden from consciousness. The manner in which we do things is repetitive. Culture, too, can be conceived of as recurring patterns in behavior and thought.

Learning a culture is similar to learning a language. Few people receive formal instruction on how to be an appropriate member of a particular cultural group. Rather, they learn by observing others, by trial, error, and continuous reinforcement. In other words, culture and language are learned affectively, not cognitively. It is not until the schooling process begins that the use of language becomes cognitive by studying spelling and grammar. As with language, it is also difficult to talk about one's culture to others who have different ways of doing things since the knowledge and vocabulary of appropriate concepts is not readily available. Only when people meet someone from a different cultural background does their own way of doing things become evident. When one extends a hand to shake upon greeting another, it is assumed that the person greeted will return the gesture. Extending a hand to greet someone from Japan, however, may elicit a bow. People are hesitant about how to respond. Assumptions about how others will behave are always present and surface quickly when they do not fulfill our expectations. People become frustrated in cross-cultural interactions because assumptions often go unfulfilled. As well, people often lack the foundation for the problems they will face when beginning to communicate with others. The result may well be intercultural miscommunication.

Teachers themselves often do not know, and generally are not taught, certain aspects of their own language and culture. Only outsiders learning a language or studying another culture need to be made aware of these recurring patterns. It may thus be difficult for teachers to teach about language and culture as few are aware of their own patterning; few ever study their own cultural conditioning. This presents another problem, for culture may best be learned affectively. Only later is the cognitive dimension put into place. Schooling, however, is typically cognition-oriented and ventures into the affective domain only rarely and only for a limited number of experiences. If the present cognitive orientation persists in schools, it will remain difficult to teach about culture in a manner effective for addressing today's needs.

The Adjustment Process

Whenever people make significant changes in their lives, they have myriad reactions, experiences, and new phenomena with which to adjust. Most people have experienced a major transition in their lives: an extended period away from home for the first time; the transition from school to work, or from work back to school or retirement; single life to married life or vice versa; a move across country; or a significant period living and working overseas or with another cultural group within one's own country.

Our world is in transition. This is evident from the shift in populations in schools around the country and the demands placed upon teachers and students who must interact over an extended period of time. When thinking about making transitions and living and working in a culturally diverse setting, we can learn a significant amount from what cross-cultural trainers have to say about the adjustment process in an international setting.

The adjustment process suggests that, as people strive to integrate themselves into a new cultural setting, they must successfully accommodate a series of predictable phases. People are initially intrigued and enraptured by the prospect of intercultural experience. Overcome with excitement, new sensations, and perceived opportunity, individuals enter what has appropriately been termed the Honeymoon Phase (Trifonovitch 1977). Early in the intercultural experience, everything seems like heaven, the new sights, places, smells, foods, dress, people, physical environment—the objective cultural differences— envelop one's experience entirely. However unknowingly, this places considerable demand upon one's physiological and psychological self. Adjusting to all that is new puts one's body in a state of constant stress and anxiety. This is exciting, though only to a point. After some time, the constant demand becomes too much, and most react to the stress by entering a state of hostility.

In the Hostility Phase, individuals have become frustrated by their inability to make sense of their new world. Where everything had initially seemed fresh and exciting, frustration arises from seemingly little things that go wrong. What was learned as right or good in the home environment does not often work well in the new setting. A different orientation toward time and space, people's values toward work and education, different use of verbal and nonverbal language, the degree to which people feel in control of their lives, and other subjective cultural differences all become evident. Many begin to take their frustration out on others in their immediate surroundings: family tensions may rise; peer relationships at work may suffer; classroom frustration may increase; or one may begin to criticize the other culture for its inability to get things done the way one feels it should. Highly ethnocentric reactions emerge at this phase, which, if not checked, may create intense interpersonal problems. This is perhaps the most critical phase of one's adjustment to working across cultures, since it is here that the subjective cultures of the two parties come into contact and potential conflicts emerge. Once one begins to understand the subjective culture of others or is able to understand why people behave as they do, one can begin to emerge from this reactive, hostile phase.

Entering the next phase, often referred to as the Humor Phase, is a positive sign. People begin to understand the subjective culture of those with whom they work and to understand the way things are perceived and accomplished in this new environment. They are able to laugh at mistakes they made in their initial reactions.

Finally, people enter the phase called Home, wherein individuals are able to interpret and interact from their own perspective as well as from that of the other cultural group. A major change occurs in the ability to process information; to understand the world in ways similar to those in the other group. The world from the other's point of view is now seen as reasonable and acceptable.

Most individuals require a significant amount of time for understanding the subtle, subjective components of another group of people in sufficient depth to work with them effectively. Some suggest as much as two years; the exact amount of time will depend upon particular individuals and circumstances.

Understanding this process has at least two important aspects. Increasing numbers of students, themselves immigrants, refugees, or temporary residents, will all experience the various stages of the adjustment process as they make the transition to a new country and culture. Teachers should expect that children, as well as their families, will confront myriad changes and personal reactions during this process. This may make it difficult for children to understand fully their new environment and attend to their schooling. Teachers—especially teachers in highly integrated settings—may also find that they require a period of adjustment to feel comfortable with and capably carry out their responsibilities. Adjustment in this case is not only one-way. Teachers, students, families, and institutions must be aware of this dynamic and expect that changes in all parties will take place.

The next major barriers to understanding others address issues related to cognition and processing information in one's environment.

Perception and Categorization

People receive millions of bits of information every day through their senses. To think that people can respond to each stimulus individually expects too much; it would severely tax their physical and emotional systems. Instead, people organize their world into groups of things that share similar characteristics; they then respond according to that category. Culture teaches one how to make sense of a busy world; in other words, how to organize the stimuli received. Sensation refers to the reception of stimuli by the senses; perception, the recognition by the brain; and categorization, to what is done with that information once it is recorded, how it is organized, and the meaning attached to it.

Some examples may enhance the understanding of the influences of culture on one's cognitive processing. Physicists tell us that the human eye can distinguish more than 8 million colors. There is no practical reason, nor is it humanly possible, even to consider the fine variations, let alone react individually to them all. People, therefore, group colors according to some scheme; the most familiar is one based on the color spectrum revealing red, orange, yellow, green, blue, and violet as the major categories. As such, when asked about the color of the sky, one's response typically is blue; a sapphire is blue, oceans are depicted on a map as blue, and so forth. Grass, however, is green, as are the leaves of most trees and the inside of a kiwi fruit.

In traditional Japanese language the term 'aoi' refers to colors that span blue and green wavelengths. When asked the color of the sky, the response would be aoi. When asked the color of grass, the response, too, would be aoi. How would you explain this? Certainly the entire Japanese population is not color-blind nor are they unable to think abstractly. Rather, whereas Euro-Americans have learned to place these particular stimuli into different categories (blue and green), the Japanese group them together.

A similar example can be made using the stimulus word 'dog'. Most Westerners consider dogs to be pets, "man's best friend," a companion, and in some cases an important member of the family. A Muslim, however, confronted by the same stimulus, would consider the dog filthy, a lowly animal, something to avoid at all costs—similar to Americans' reaction to a pig. Some Filipinos or Pacific Islanders on the other hand would place the dog in the food category. It is not uncommon to find dog meat as part of the diet in many homes in that part of the world.

Although the same stimuli impinge upon all people, one's culture determines what sense one makes of the world. What happens when one observes or interacts with someone who categorizes the world differently or behaves in a manner distinct from that to which one is accustomed? This leads to the next barrier to learning about others: the judgments people make.

The Attribution Process

People make judgments about others based on behavior they observe. They judge others competent or not, educated or naive, well-intentioned or ill-intentioned, and so forth. Psychologists call these judgments attributions. Unfortunately, human thinking is fallible; people often judge others differently from the way they judge themselves. For instance, when people fail at a given task, they are likely to look for blame in the situation, not in themselves. They may blame failure on a recent bout with the flu, heavy traffic they encountered on their way to work, or a difficult work schedule. However, when one observes another's failure, the tendency is to place a trait label on that person as lazy, uneducated, ill-mannered, and so forth. These trait labels often become negative stereotypes of the group. This may lead on to the categorization process—the need people have to simplify things in their lives and the tendency to respond to things according to the category, ignoring individual traits. Stereotyping, a naturally occurring cognitive response in humans, results in forming categories for people. Because a specific culture teaches people to categorize other cultures as positive and negative, most stereotypes end up by placing negative labels upon groups of people.

A school-based example that might occur between black or Hispanic students and white teachers may help explain the attribution process. Many black and Hispanic children are taught that it is disrespectful to look a person of authority in the eye especially when being reprimanded. Instead, one demonstrates respect by looking down and away from the direct stare of the adult. White teachers, on the contrary, may expect a child who is being reprimanded to look directly at them. In a classroom situation where a white teacher scolds a black or Hispanic child, a white teacher would likely make the misattribution that a child was disrespectful for failing to look the teacher directly in the eye, whereas, in reality, black or Hispanic children would be showing respect in the manner they were taught; it is the white teacher who misread the cues and misjudged the child.

Effective intercultural communication occurs when both parties of an interaction suspend judgment, seek to understand the reasons behind another's actions, and then become able to explain another's behavior according to its intent. The goal of making mutual attributions that is, to have both individuals in an exchange explain the causes of each other's behavior in the same way — is not unreasonable. When this occurs, misunderstanding and miscommunication can be reduced. People frequently cannot explain their own behavior. Children, especially, do not know that they are expected to look or not to look the teacher in the eye. In the example, the effective teacher would understand that the child demonstrates respect by avoiding looking directly at the teacher. To attempt to make isomorphic attribution may avoid further problems. Cross-cultural attribution training has demonstrated the ability to change significantly people's cognitive, affective, and behavioral processes.

Summary and Conclusions

Although they are not the focus of this paper, we know that effective cross-cultural training strategies and activities to break down cultural barriers within the school context exist. Slavin's (1979) cooperative learning research demonstrated the application of concepts from the intergroup interaction literature to instructional design in the classroom. Brislin, Cushner, Cherrie, and Yong's (1986) culture-general training strategy has been effective in increasing knowledge and understanding cross-cultural interaction among preservice teachers (Ilola 1988). In addition, this approach has increased knowledge and understanding of cross-cultural concepts and improved problem-solving strategies among high school students (Cushner 1989). Many other effective classroom activities designed to improve intercultural interaction and understanding are available that can easily be integrated in the curriculum.

Today's complex, interdependent world demands that individuals be able to work with a diversity of people to solve their own and the world's problems. This requires attaining an ethnorelative perspective, an expectation that one will have significant adjustments to make when working and living with others, as well as an ability to understand components of one's own and others' subjective culture. Individuals acquire a subjective culture unique to a particular group as a result of being socialized in a given manner. Components of subjective culture include, but are not limited to, the manner by which persons learn, the way they categorize the world around them, and the attributions they make about the behavior of others. Because we all are cultural beings, certain behaviors, attitudes, and perspectives we exhibit may become barriers in our quest to learn about others. Knowledge of these potential obstacles and attention to educating ourselves and others about these will, in the long run, help to eliminate anxieties and to encourage effective intercultural interaction.

Activity 14

Adjustment to Change

Purpose

To identify the emotional responses that can occur during a major transition experience, and relate them to international and/or intercultural adjustment.

Instructions

Think back to the discussion of the U-Curve hypothesis and people's adaptation to change in the previous article. What major transitions have you had in your life? Identify one that extended over a rather lengthy period of time. Perhaps you moved to another state, another section of town, or a new neighborhood within your town or city. Perhaps you recall beginning a new school, going to summer camp, or moving into a dormitory as a freshman in college. Draw a graph in the space below that traces out your emotional responses during that experience from the time when you first began the experience until the time when you felt completely "at home."

My Transition Experience

```
h
i
g
h

E
M
O
T
I
O
N
S

l
o
w
```
                                    time

What phases of your experience reflect ones that are similar to the U-Curve hypothesis?

_____

_____

_____

_____

_____

_____

To what do you attribute major changes in your graph? What helped you overcome any difficulties you may have encountered?

_____

_____

_____

_____

_____

What would you suggest to others as they encounter similar major adjustments in their lives?

_____

_____

_____

_____

_____

How might you use this experience to prepare you for significant cross-cultural encounters?

_____

_____

_____

_____

How might the adjustment process be evident in schools for students? For teachers? For parents?

For students:

_____

_____

_____

_____

_____

_____

_____

_____

For teachers:

_____

_____

_____

_____

_____

_____

For parents:

_____

_____

_____

_____

_____

_____

A Culture-General Framework for Understanding Intercultural Interactions

Purpose

To identify concepts that cut across diversity and have an impact on interpersonal interactions in the school, classroom and community.

Instructions

Read the following content and respond to the reflective questions that follow.

It is rather difficult to think about preparing people to interact with others of any specific culture given the diversity of most schools and communities in the United States. Fortunately, researchers in the fields of cross-cultural psychology and intercultural training have identified concepts and experiences people are certain to confront regardless of their own background, the cultures with which they are interacting, and their particular role in the new cultural setting. This model, presented by Cushner and Brislin (1996) and referred to as the *18-Theme Culture-General Framework,* is presented below. Because this model is deliberately general, its usefulness lies in its adaptability to any cross-cultural encounter. This model allows us to capture the experience of cultural differences from a variety of perspectives (emotional, informational, and developmental), and to offer frameworks within which specific problem situations can be addressed.

Stage One: Understanding Emotional Responses in Intercultural Interaction

In any intercultural encounter, people's emotions are quickly aroused when they meet with unpredictable behavior on the part of others or when their own behavior does not bring about anticipated responses. It is important to note that the nature and strength of these emotional reactions quite often surprises the people involved. This is often the case with students from some backgrounds who may not have anticipated the differences between their own culture and that of the school. It is also the case for teachers who find themselves in a school or classroom context that is significantly different from their prior experience. Recognizing, understanding and accommodating the strong emotional responses people are certain to have when involved in intercultural interactions is critical to successfully negotiating them. Below is a list of the emotional responses people most often confront when interacting with an unfamiliar culture. A brief discussion of these responses follows.

Anxiety
Ambiguity
Disconfirmed Expectations
Belonging/Rejection
Confronting Personal Prejudice

Anxiety: As individuals encounter unexpected or unfamiliar behavior of others, they are likely to become anxious about whether or not their own behavior is appropriate. Children in new schools, families in new communities, and teachers in new schools will all experience some degree of anxiety as they attempt to modify their own behavior to fit the new circumstances. Feelings of anxiety may result in a strong desire to avoid the situation altogether and individuals sometimes go to great lengths to do so, all the while rationalizing their avoidance behavior on other grounds.

Can you think of times when **anxiety** was evident in your life and how it might have interfered with your ability to function most effectively?

_____

_____

_____

_____

_____

Ambiguity: When interacting with those who are culturally different, the messages received from the other person are often unclear, yet decisions have to be made and appropriate behavior somehow produced. Most people, when faced with an ambiguous situation, try to resolve it by applying culturally familiar criteria. People who are effective at working across cultures are known to have a high tolerance for ambiguity. That is, in situations where they do not have full understanding of what is going on, they are skilled at asking appropriate questions and modifying their behavior accordingly.

Can you recall times when things have been **ambiguous**, unclear, or uncomfortable for you, yet you still had to function? What did you do that helped you to do what needed to be done?

_____

_____

_____

_____

Disconfirmed Expectations: Individuals may become upset or uncomfortable, not because of the specific circumstances they encounter but because the situation differs from what they expect. Despite our recognition that differences are all around us, we have a tendency to expect others to think and behave in ways similar to ourselves. Most people enter into interactions with others expecting that others will think and behave according to preconceived, often inaccurate, notions. They then act on those inaccurate judgments, and find that their actions do not produce the intended result.

Can you recall a time when you experienced **disconfirmed expectations** and thought the situation would be one way when in fact it was quite different? How did you reconcile this difference?

_____

_____

_____

_____

Belonging/Rejection: People have a need to fill a social niche, to feel that they "belong," and are "at home" in the social milieu in which they find themselves. When people are immersed in an intercultural interaction this sense of belonging may be difficult to achieve because they don't know the "rules" of behavior in the new situation. Rather, they often feel rejected as an "outsider". When this sense of rejection is strong enough they may become alienated from the situation altogether. Students, for example, who may feel alienated from the classroom or school, are more likely to become discipline problems and have difficulty paying attention to classroom work.

Can you recall a time when you felt as if you did not **belong**? How did this make you feel? How did you respond? What might you suggest to another who has similar feelings?

_____

_____

_____

_____

Confronting Personal Prejudice: Finally, when involved in cross-cultural interactions, one may be forced to acknowledge that previously held beliefs about a certain group of people or certain kinds of behaviors may be inaccurate or without foundation. Such a revelation may result in embarrassment or shame. It may also require a basic change in one's attitude and behavior toward others. And, since change is difficult even in the best of circumstances, people often continue to harbor their prejudices even when faced with contradictory evidence.

Can you think of **prejudices** you might harbor about certain people? Can you think of a time or times when you found that information that you held about certain people was not accurate or true?

_____

_____

_____

_____

_____

_____

Stage Two: Understanding the Cultural Basis of Unfamiliar Behavior

In addition to accommodating their feelings, both parties in an intercultural encounter need to understand the cultural influences that direct one another's knowledge base as a means of understanding one another's behavior. Individuals typically try to understand another person's behavior according to their own cultural patterns. Put another way, since most people do not have extensive experiences with people who think and act differently from themselves, they tend to interpret another's behavior in terms of their own cultural frame of reference. In brief, we see what we expect to see, and with incomplete information or inaccurate knowledge, we may make inappropriate judgments about a given situation.

A relatively common example may illustrate this point. Some children from certain cultural groups (e.g., some, but certainly not all, Latino and African-Americans) are taught to demonstrate respect for elders or persons in authority by avoiding eye contact. Hence a child being reprimanded by a parent or teacher may avoid gazing in that person's eyes. On the other hand, most European-American children (who end up being the majority of the teachers in schools) are taught to look a person of authority directly in the eye. Imagine the outcome of an interaction involving an African-American or Latino child being reprimanded by a European-American teacher. The child, as she or he has been taught, may look away from the gaze of the teacher thereby demonstrating respect. The teacher, expecting eye contact as a sign of respect, interprets the child's behavior as suggesting that "He or she is not listening to me," or "This child does not respect me." This incorrect judgment may jeopardize future interactions between this particular teacher, student, and family.

The individual skilled in intercultural encounters learns to seek alternative explanations of unexpected behavior rather than simply interpreting such behavior according to his or her own cultural framework. The question, "Why is this behavior occurring?" precedes the question, "What is the matter with this child?"

There are many components of cultural knowledge, each of which reaches the individual through a network of socializing agents. Regardless of the complexity of this socialization process, the resulting knowledge base functions to give us satisfactory explanations of the world, and tells us how best to interact with other people. Within this knowledge base, however, the following kinds of knowledge are likely to differ across cultures.

Communication and Language Use
Values
Rituals and Superstition
Situational Behavior
Roles
Social Status
Time and Space
Group versus the Individual

Communication and Language Use. Communication differences are probably the most obvious problem to be overcome when crossing cultural boundaries. This is the case whether the **languages** involved are completely different (e.g., Japanese, Kiswahili, English, American Sign Language), are similar in root but not in evolution (e.g., French, Italian, Spanish), or are variations or dialects of the same language (e.g., French and French-Canadian, English and Ebonics). In any case, many people find it difficult to learn a second (or third) language. In addition, **nonverbal communication** customs such as facial expressions, gestures, and so forth, also differ across cultures so that what a particular gesture means to one person may have a very different meaning to someone from another culture.

Can you think of instances where you have encountered **communication** difference, both verbal as well as nonverbal?

_____

_____

_____

_____

_____

Values: The development of internalized values is one of the chief socialization goals in all societies. Values provide social cohesion among group members and are often codified into laws or rules for living, such as the Ten Commandments for Christians and Jews or the Hippocratic Oath for doctors. The range of possible values with respect to any particular issue is usually wide, deeply held, and often difficult to change. For example, in the dominant culture of the United States, belief in "progress" is highly valued and almost religious in character. A teacher subscribing to that value may have a very difficult time interacting with the parents of a young woman who seems not to value her academic potential. The young woman's parents may believe that she should assume the traditional role of wife and mother after high school rather than seek a college education. The teacher, on the other hand, may believe that the young woman should "look to the future," "change with the times," and "make progress" for herself. These are not small differences.

Can you recall instances where **value differences** came between you and someone else? How did you reconcile these differences?

_____

_____

_____

_____

_____

Ritual and Superstitions: All social groups develop **rituals** that help members meet the demands of everyday life. Such rituals vary in significance from rubbing a rabbit's foot before a stressful event to the intricate format of an organized religious service. The difficulty, however, is that the rituals of one culture may be viewed as **superstitions** by members of other cultures. Increasingly, children from a wide variety of religious and cultural backgrounds bring to school behaviors that are often misunderstood and labeled "superstitious" by others in the school or community.

Can you think of instances where one person's **rituals** may be interpreted by others to be **superstitious**, and might be evident in the school context?

_____

_____

_____

_____

_____

Situational Behavior: Knowing how to behave appropriately in a variety of settings and situations is important to all people. The **"rules" for behavior** in a particular context are internalized at an early age and can be easily perceived to be "broken" by one who has internalized a different set of rules for the same setting or situation. Examples of this can be found in the workplace, in social settings, in schools, when making decisions and solving problems, and deciding whom one should turn to in time of need.

Can you think of instances where the rules and **behavior** you thought were appropriate to follow were not expected in a certain context? How did you react? What did you do to resolve the difference?

_____

_____

_____

_____

_____

Role: Knowledge of appropriate **role behavior**, like that of situational behavior, may vary from role to role and from group to group. How one behaves as a mother or father, for example, may be different from how one behaves as a teacher. Likewise, gender- and age-related behavior between groups may also differ in a significant manner.

Can you think of examples of how certain **role-based behavior** might differ across cultures?

_____

_____

_____

_____

_____

Social Status: All social groups make distinctions based on markers of high and low status. **Social class** and **social status** are both the results of stratification systems, whose role assignments may vary considerably from group to group. The role of "aunt" in the African-American community has a much higher status than it does in middle-class, European-American society. For example, the aunt of an African-American child may bear considerable responsibility for the well-being of that child. Middle-class European-American teachers, when confronted by a very pro-active aunt and unaware of this status and relationship, may believe that the child's mother is somehow shirking her duties.

Can you think of instances where you might have misinterpreted a given person's **status**? What kinds of problems might this have caused?

_____

_____

_____

_____

_____

Time and Space: Differences in conceptions of time and space may also vary among social groups. In addition to differences in the divisions of **time** (e.g., a week, a crop harvest), groups vary in the degree to which time is valued. It is common for European-Americans, for example, to value punctuality since that is seen as an expression of respect. However, measures of time and their value may be much more elastic in less-industrialized societies where work is less synchronized. Similarly, the ease and comfort of one's **position in space** vis-a-vis other people may vary. How close one stands to another when speaking, and the degree to which one should stand face-to-face with another are both subject to cultural variation.

Can you recall instances where your concept of **time** differed in a significant way from another person? Can you think of instances when another's use of **space** seemed to interfere with yours?

_____

_____

_____

_____

Relationship to the group versus the individual: All people sometimes act according to their **individual interests** and sometimes according to their **group allegiances**. The relative emphasis on group versus individual orientation varies from group to group and may significantly affect the choices one makes. People from more collective societies, for instance, may defer decision making to other elders or relatives. People from more individualistic societies, on the other hand, may be socialized to make most decisions pretty much on their own.

Can you think of instances when people were responding more to the **collective** or **group** when you would have done otherwise? Or, when people stood more on their own when you would have expected them to look to others for guidance and support?

_____

_____

_____

_____

Stage Three: Making Adjustments and Reshaping Cultural Identity

Finally, as a result of prolonged intercultural interactions, an individual may experience profound personal change. That is, an individual's way of perceiving the world, processing those perceptions, and viewing themselves as well as others may alter. Typically, for example, individuals who have had significant intercultural experiences become more complex thinkers. This is, of course, one of the central goals of multicultural education since it enables people to handle more culturally complex stimuli, to be accurate in their interpretations of others' behavior, and thus to deal more effectively with the differences they encounter. As individuals continue to have intercultural experiences, they become less culture-bound and more understanding of how others perceive the world. Such individuals can now "see" from another point of view; they are more complex thinkers and can handle a greater variety of diverse information. They are also less likely to make inaccurate judgments or attributions because they are more likely to inquire into behavior and beliefs they do not comprehend, thereby improving their understanding. Think back to the gaze-avoidance behavior in the interaction between the European-American teacher and the Latino or African-American child referred to earlier. The interculturally knowledgeable teacher would understand the meaning behind the child's gaze-avoidance and thus more accurately judge the child to be listening and demonstrating respect. While one may have limited knowledge of the content of other cultures, we know that all people *process information* in similar ways. Important ways of processing information are listed below, each of which can be investigated by the participants in intercultural exchanges.

Categorization
Differentiation
Attribution
Ingroups-Outgroups
Learning Style

Categorization: Since people cannot attend to all the information presented to them, they create **categories** for organizing and responding to similar bits of information. Cultural stereotypes, for example, are categories usually associated with particular groups of people. People involved in intercultural interactions often categorize one another quickly according to whatever category systems they have learned.

Can you think of situations where miscategorization was evident; that is, when one person or group of people **categorized** certain information in one manner while another individual or group **categorized** it differently?

_____

_____

_____

_____

Differentiation: Information related to highly meaningful categories becomes more highly refined or **differentiated**. As a result, new categories may be formed. Such refinement or differentiation is usually shared only among people who have had many experiences in common (e.g., doctors) and thus may be unknown even to those whose general background is similar. A good example of this process is the way in which people in Asia might differentiate the food 'rice.' Because it is an extremely important part of their diet it can be referred to in many different ways, by many different terms, and can have many different uses. For most European-Americans, rice is not as important and, thus, fewer references are made to it. Or, consider students in a particular high school who differentiate their peers into groups such as "brains," "nerds," "jocks," etc. While a similar type of differentiation may occur in most high schools, the particular categories and their meaning may differ considerably from school to school.

Can you think of other elements in your culture that are highly **differentiated** but may not be so highly differentiated by others? Or, can you think of examples of an element from another culture that is highly differentiated but is not so important in your own group?

_____

_____

_____

_____

_____

Attribution: People not only perceive others according to familiar categories, they also make judgments about others based on the behavior they observe. People judge others, for example, as competent or incompetent, educated or naive, well-intentioned or ill-intentioned. Psychologists call these judgments **attributions,** and tell us that within about seven seconds of meeting someone new, initial judgments are made. These initial 'sizing-up' judgments, once made, are usually quite resistant to change. Human judgments, however, are fallible, and certain errors occur repeatedly in human thought. One of these, called the **fundamental attribution error**, describes the tendency people have to judge others on different sets of criteria than they apply to themselves. Thus, if a person fails at a given task, he or she is more likely to look to the situation for an explanation: it was too hot, someone else was unfair to the person, the task was unreasonable. If a person observes someone else fail at a task, he or she is more likely to explain the failure in terms of the other person's traits: she is lazy, he is stupid, she is uncaring. This tendency is even more prevalent in cross-cultural situations because there is so much behavior that is unfamiliar. Given the speed with which people make judgments and the probable lack of intercultural understanding, attribution errors abound in intercultural situations.

Can you provide examples when you may have judged a situation differently from that of someone else? Or, can you think of a time when someone made an inaccurate **attribution** about you that differed from how you would have judged yourself?

_____

_____

_____

_____

_____

Ingroups and Outgroups: People the world over divide others into groups with which they are comfortable and can discuss their concerns (**ingroups**) and those who are kept at a distance (**outgroups**), oftentimes based on their own system of categorization and differentiation. Those entering new cultural situations must recognize that they will often be considered members of the outgroup and will not share certain ingroup behavior and communication, at least at the outset. As a result, people may be kept from participating in certain ingroup activities, such as may happen when workmates get together on Friday after a week of work.

Can you think of a situation where you thought you would be included in the **ingroup** but were not, or, when you got together with your ingroup and others were left out? Can you think of times when others might be excluded for no other reason than they were not considered a part of a particular ingroup?

_____

_____

_____

_____

_____

Learning style: Sometimes called cognitive style, this refers to one's **preferred method of learning** and is very much under cultures' influence. How (and what) one perceives, the categories into which one places sensory stimuli, and whether learning is preferred through observation, listening, or action are all, in part, culturally-based. Learning styles are partly the result of strengths and weaknesses in sensory perception (one's hearing may be more acute than one's vision, for example). However, it is also the case that cultural patterning may teach a child to attend to certain kinds of stimuli rather than others, as when children from collectivist societies learn better in cooperative groups.

Can you think of culturally-based examples of where one's **learning style** might be in conflict with the teaching style of the teacher?

_____

_____

_____

_____

_____

_____

_____

_____

_____

_____

_____

_____

_____

_____

_____

_____

_____

Critical Incident Review

Purpose

To apply the 18-theme culture general framework to critical incidents in a school context.

Instructions

Let's imagine what might happen in any intercultural interchange. People have certain expectations of the outcomes of their own behavior as well as the motivations of others. And, as discussed in the previous exercise, people have a tendency to make judgments or attributions about others based upon the behavior they observe. Such expectations come primarily from their own socialization, predisposing them to view the world from one particular perspective. When people's expectations are not met, they must reconcile the difference between the reality and their expectations (**disconfirmed expectations**). Such is the basis of the strong emotional reaction in cultural conflict. Many outcomes are possible, including:

> People feel extreme emotional upset, oftentimes without knowing what is at play (remember, culture is a secret!). As such, they may have a tendency to avoid further cross-cultural encounters, as they are perceived as unpleasant;

and/or

> People may make **faulty attributions**, or assign inaccurate interpretations to the meaning and intentions of one's behavior, accusing her or him of lacking sufficient knowledge, cheating, being pushy—in other words, interpreting events from their own ethnocentric perspective and thus judging others by inappropriate standards;

and/or

> People may begin to inquire as to how others interpret or find meaning in their world. As people begin to learn how others understand and operate from their own perspective or subjective culture, true culture learning begins to take place. This suggests that people have a need to broaden their knowledge base about others, about their own socialization, as well as that of others.

The culture-general framework provides one such foundation of knowledge concerning issues at play in intercultural interaction. Building such a knowledge base enables individuals to understand and overcome the oftentimes unexpected but strong emotions they are certain to encounter in themselves; to be more precise and accurate in their interpretations of other's behavior; and thus, to interact more effectively with those different from themselves.

Following are a number of critical incidents designed to help you develop a foundation in the culture-general framework. Read each incident, respond to the questions that immediately follow, and select the alternative that best explains the situation. Feedback on your responses are provided at the end of this section, pages 137–145.

An alternative strategy for working with critical incidents is to do the following in small groups:

1. Read and discuss one incident. Be certain all understand the situation.
2. Rank in order the alternative explanations. Which can you agree are probably the most insightful explanations?
3. Then, read the rationales that provide feedback on your choices.
4. Identify which of the 18 culture-general themes you think help one to understand the situation.
5. Relate the theme(s) to your own experience and/or to an educational setting. How have you observed this theme in action? How do you think it might be present in various classroom settings?

A Model Minority

Wellington Chang was a sixth-grade student in a San Francisco neighborhood elementary school. Recently arrived from Hong Kong, he spoke very functional, though accented, English.

His sixth-grade class was multiethnic with students of African American, Latino, and various Asian backgrounds, as well as a few European Americans. His teacher, Mr. Fenwick, was a competent teacher with more than 25 years experience in the classroom. Of German heritage, Mr. Fenwick had watched as the district's population was transformed into an incredibly heterogeneous mixture of ethnic and linguistic groups. He prided himself on his ability to adapt to the ever-changing and complex environment.

Though Wellington seemed quiet enough at first, he increasingly exhibited what Mr. Fenwick described as disruptive behavior, including talking, laughing, and teasing other students. This perplexed Mr. Fenwick since his experience with Chinese young people was that they were among the most hard-working and diligent students. Far from being disruptive, Mr. Fenwick found most Chinese students to be relatively passive individuals whom he had to encourage to be more participatory. Thus Wellington's behavior seemed to him particularly disturbing and he punished him more severely than other non-Chinese students, even though his behavior was no worse than theirs. The principal noticed this discrepancy during a recent observation and brought it to Mr. Fenwick's attention.

If you were the principal, how would you address this with Mr. Fenwick? From the 18-theme culture-general framework, what issues might be operating unconsciously to explain Mr. Fenwick's behavior?

_____

_____

_____

_____

_____

_____

Now, given the following alternatives, which provides the most insight into the situation?

1. Mr. Fenwick believes that no matter where they come from, all Chinese will behave in the same manner.
2. Mr. Fenwick is operating from very limited experience with ethnic minorities in the United States and does not realize that Wellington's behavior is well within the normal range for U.S. sixth-graders, regardless of their background.
3. Mr. Fenwick's expectations about the Chinese being a model minority cause him to judge Wellington too harshly.
4. For some reason, Mr. Fenwick has taken a personal dislike to Wellington.

Feedback on these alternatives can be found on page 137

The Proposal Process

The principal at Wilson High called a staff meeting for all social studies personnel to discuss upcoming curricular changes. Stu Abrams, a social studies teacher for 11 years, reread some materials he wished to see incorporated into the program in which he taught. In particular, he was looking forward to integrating a new set of multicultural materials into the program. For a long time he had felt the district was ignoring the influx of Filipino, Vietnamese, and Samoan immigrants into the community. It was about time for change.

Jose, a second-generation Filipino teacher, was also asked to attend the meeting. Jose had developed a close relationship with Stu, and they were to work on this committee together. They had worked on many other projects together. The principal asked Stu to review his proposal, the substance of which was already known to the others at the meeting. The proposal went through with little modification and it was agreed to take the next step toward eventual implementation. Since this had taken less time than expected, the principal asked Jose to say a few words about the curriculum development project he had been working on. Again, most of the people at the meeting knew of this project. Jose gave an outline of his thinking, and Stu then asked some rather difficult questions that forced Jose to think on his feet and to defend some of his earlier assumptions. When the principal ended the meeting, Jose, seemingly quite upset, said that he preferred not to work on the committee with Stu as originally planned. The principal was puzzled.

What insights can you provide into the reason why Jose asked to be removed from Stu's committee? From the 18-theme culture-general framework, what issues might be operating that help to explain Jose's response?

_____

_____

_____

_____

_____

_____

_____

Now, which of the following alternatives provides the most insight?

1. Jose wanted to do some additional work on his own proposal and see it ultimately adopted by the group.
2. Jose was jealous that Stu's proposal had passed on to the next step with little modification.
3. Jose felt that Stu withdrew his friendship at the meeting.
4. Jose felt that he, being an ethnic minority himself, should have his suggestions adopted.

Feedback on these alternatives can be found on page 137

Typical American Practice

"Class, I'd like you to welcome Keiko, an exchange student from Japan, who will be attending Central High School for the second semester," said Mr. Cooper at the beginning of his American Government class. Keiko had experienced similar introductions and welcomes in all of her classes during her first day of school in the United States. The friendliness of the faculty and students impressed her and made her feel right at home.

As time went on, however, Keiko felt that the teachers and students were ignoring her more and more. Very few students talked to her, and only offered a brief hello in the hallway or cafeteria. Some students, and even families, after talking with her for a while, left saying things like, "We'll have to get together some time," or, "I'll call you soon." This rarely seemed to happen, however. And although Keiko received mostly A's in class, her teachers hardly ever called on her in class. She began to wonder if she had somehow offended the people at her new school, and she gradually became withdrawn and isolated.

What do you think has happened here to cause this unfortunate situation? From the 18-theme culture-general framework, what issues might be operating to explain the situation?

_____

_____

_____

_____

_____

_____

_____

_____

_____

_____

Given the following alternatives, which would you select as most appropriate?

1. The students resent Keiko's high grades and are showing their jealousy of her.
2. Americans have a tendency to offer foreigners a special welcome and then quickly treat them like everyone else.
3. Keiko demands too much attention and has unrealistic expectations that everyone will treat her in a special way.
4. The faculty members are obviously insincere in their initial welcomes. They are probably acting on a directive from the principal.

Feedback on these alternatives can be found on page 138

The Students Are Anxious, but Why?

It was test week throughout the city, and teachers and parents were anxious how things would go this time around. In previous years the district's scores were among the lowest in the state, and the city government had considered taking over the school system.

Today, Mary McConnell was exhausted! Normally she could cope with the challenges of being homeroom teacher for ninth graders, but today had been extremely difficult. All morning her students had taken standardized tests and they had been "impossible." They had taken a long time to settle down in their seats; everyone had to sharpen their two required pencils, and halfway through the process, the pencil sharpener had mysteriously broken.

One boy just would not stop talking and cracking jokes from the back of the room. He was often encouraged by remarks and giggles from the girls around him. Two girls had flatly refused to take the tests, and Ms. McConnell had sent them to the principal's office. Three students had marked their answer sheets in patterns without even reading the questions. Ms. McConnell had tried to enlist the students' genuine participation, but they had refused. Two of them then put their heads down on their desks and would not respond to her at all.

Mary McConnell knew she was facing a high level of resistance in the room. However, she could not understand what was going on. Can you? What would you recommend she do? From the 18-theme culture-general framework, what issues might be operating to explain the circumstances?

Of the four alternatives below, select the response that, to you, best explains the situation.

1. The students were very anxious because they didn't like the strict time limits of standardized tests.
2. These students had scored low on standardized tests in past years and because they expected to do so again, felt quite anxious.
3. When the pencil sharpener broke and the students couldn't sharpen their pencils, they became anxious about marking their answer sheets correctly.
4. The students did not like their daily classroom routine interrupted by such a long activity.

Feedback on these alternatives can be found on page 139

Saving Face

Mrs. McMillen teaches an advanced-level course in Algebra-Trigonometry. Her class of 20 has some of the school's top students. For the first grading period, one of her students, a 16-year-old from India who is in his first year of U.S. education, received a B. The day after report cards were issued this student's father requested an immediate meeting with the principal. At the meeting the father was obviously quite upset with his son's grade because his son had always achieved A's and at his previous school had led last year's honor roll with a perfect 4.0 grade-point average.

The principal explained that, according to Mrs. McMillen, the student had earned a C on one particularly difficult test, causing his average to drop to a B. He also stated that Mrs. McMillen had said that the boy was one of her best students and that he could still get an A in the course by the end of the semester.

At the end of the meeting, the father announced that he wanted his son transferred from the advanced level of the course to the regular level of the course. The principal asked the father to postpone his request for one day while he considered the situation further.

What would you suggest the principal do to help resolve this problem? From the 18-theme culture-general framework, what issues might be operating to help explain the father's behavior?

Now, of the four alternatives below, which do you think was actually enacted as the best solution to this situation?

1. Realizing the importance of this student's grades to the father, the principal should talk to Mrs. McMillen to see if there is some way to justify changing the grade to an A.
2. Refuse to discuss the issue any further and tell the father to stop interfering in his son's education.
3. Collect all the student's homework and tests and point out all shortcomings to the father.
4. Talk to the student privately and encourage him to try to reason with his father.

Feedback on these alternatives can be found on page 139

The Art Awards Ceremony

Tony, an African American high school student, had an interest in art that he pursued on his own by visiting museums, reading books, sketching, and painting. Much of his work reflected his African American heritage. Tony enrolled at midterm in the predominantly white JFK High School. He took an art class and was encouraged by his teacher to develop his talent. Tony entered several paintings in the school art show, received praise and attention for his work, and went on to enter the all city show, where he also did well. The longtime principal of his school, a middle-aged European American, Mr. Tarbell, was present at the awards ceremony and was delighted that one of his students received rave reviews and an award. Congratulating Tony he said, "Good work, Tony. We are proud to have such a talented black student representing our school. You have an uncanny ability to paint."

Mr. Tarbell was surprised when Tony simply walked away from him with no comment.

What do you think is going on in this incident? From the 18-theme culture-general framework, what issues might help to explain Tony's behavior?

_____

_____

_____

_____

_____

_____

_____

_____

_____

_____

Of the following explanations, how might this behavior best be interpreted?

1. Tony was overwhelmed by all the attention and uncomfortable around someone in Mr. Tarbell's position.
2. Tony was offended by what Mr. Tarbell said.
3. Tony's friends likely motioned for him to come join them. Caught up in the excitement, he simply went on over to them.
4. Tony, embarrassed and not used to the praise he was receiving, especially from the school administration, left feeling uncomfortable.

Feedback on these alternatives can be found on page 140

The Missed Meeting

Mrs. Conant, an 11th grade social studies teacher, was concerned that a newly arrived Lebanese student, Rema, was having difficulty in dealing with the material in her U.S. History textbook. After Rema failed two consecutive tests, Mrs. Conant called Rema's parents and arranged a conference for 9:45 a.m. on Thursday during her free period.

Before school on Thursday, Mrs. Conant prepared a list of her questions, concerns, and recommendations regarding Rema and was looking forward to meeting the parents. After teaching her first class, she made certain that the central office secretary would direct the couple to her room, and then she returned there at 9:30 to await their arrival. As 9:45, and then 10:00 passed and no one showed, Mrs. Conant became increasingly puzzled and irritated.

When the clock read 10:10, Mrs. Conant assumed the parents had forgotten about the appointment or had experienced car trouble. She, therefore, decided to spend the remainder of her free period in the faculty lounge. On her way out the door, however, she met the parents, who introduced themselves and said how happy they were to have the opportunity to discuss their daughter's progress. They made no mention of their lateness and offered no apology or explanation.

Mrs. Conant, trying to hide her anger, told them that she had only a few minutes left and tersely explained her perceptions of Rema's difficulties. When the parents began to give some feedback, the bell rang for the next class. Mrs. Conant cut them off, explaining that she had another class to teach. The parents, looking confused and insulted, left an angry Mrs. Conant returning to teach her class.

What would you say is the best explanation of the underlying problem of this unfortunate incident? From the 18-theme culture-general framework, what issue may be operating?

_____

_____

_____

_____

_____

_____

Now, of the following alternative explanations, which do you think best explains the cultural difference that may be operating?

1. Mrs. Conant was overly concerned about Rema's minor academic problems. A conference was really unnecessary, and the parents felt resentful about being summoned to school and didn't really want to come in the first place.

2. The parents were obviously at fault for being so late. Their lack of consideration for a teacher's valuable time indicates they are just not very concerned about their daughter or the feelings of others.

3. The parents and Mrs. Conant differ in their outlook on time and punctuality. Being 20 to 25 minutes late was no big deal to the parents, but it was very important to the teacher.

4. Mrs. Conant resents having to give up her free period to have parent-teacher conferences.

Feedback on these alternatives can be found on page 140

Bad Calls on the Tennis Court

Pitchit is a 16-year-old Thai student who has been attending high school in Dallas for the last year and a half. He tried out for the tennis team, and because of his obvious talent he earned a spot on the team as the second singles player. Coach Butler was impressed with Pitchit's play and the 7-1 record he had compiled.

During a match against one of the area's better players, Coach Butler watched as Pitchit won the first set 6-3. Figuring that Pitchit would win the match easily, Mr. Butler went to another court to watch one of his doubles teams play. Later he was surprised to learn that Pitchit lost the next two sets and the match. Another member of the team told Mr. Butler that Pitchit's opponent made many bad line calls at crucial points in the match. He said that Pitchit knew he was being cheated, but he did not protest or challenge his opponent in any way. When the coach asked Pitchit about the match and why he did not stand up to his opponent's cheating, Pitchit said, "I just got beat; that's all."

Why do you think Pitchit acted the way that he did? From the 18-theme culture-general framework, what issues might be operating that shed light on Pitchit's behavior?

_____

_____

_____

_____

_____

_____

_____

_____

How can Pitchit's reaction to an obvious injustice be explained?

1. Pitchit does not think winning is such a big deal.
2. Pitchit knows that he really lacks the talent to be the team's second singles player.
3. Pitchit resents the fact that Coach Butler did not watch his entire match.
4. Pitchit was not assertive enough to confront his opponent about the bad line call.

Feedback on these alternatives can be found on page 141

What Happened to Mariko?

Mr. Simms, chemistry teacher and moderator of the junior class, needed two more students to help as guides and hosts for the school's science fair. While walking through the cafeteria, he saw two of his better students, Julie and Mariko, an exchange student from Japan. When he asked them about helping at the fair, Julie responded with an enthusiastic, "Yes." Mariko, however, hesitated and said that she felt her English was not good enough. Both Mr. Simms and Julie assured Mariko that her English was excellent and that she would do well as a guide. Mariko still appeared very hesitant, but said nothing else as Mr. Simms told the girls when to arrive at the fair on Saturday.

On the day of the fair, Mariko failed to show up. Mr. Simms and Julie were surprised and puzzled. On the following Monday Mr. Simms asked Mariko what happened. Mariko was vague and evasive, replying that she "just couldn't make it on Saturday."

What do you think is the reason Mariko didn't show up? Which of the 18 culture-general themes might provide insight into this situation?

_____

_____

_____

_____

_____

_____

_____

_____

_____

_____

Now, of the following alternatives, which is the most plausible explanation for Mariko's behavior?

1. Mariko resented being railroaded into going to the fair and not having the opportunity to explain why she was unable to attend.
2. Mariko was reluctant to refuse the teacher's request because it would seem impolite and disrespectful.
3. Mariko felt that Mr. Simms and Julie were going out of their way to be kind to her. This caused her to feel embarrassed and somewhat angry. She was too proud to accept the extra help and attention they were offering.
4. Mariko felt that since the fair was not during school time, she had no obligation to attend or to explain why she was not there.

Feedback on these alternatives can be found on page 141

Conversation at Lunch

Ranjani and Sathie, two female students from India studying at a large Midwestern university, often eat lunch together in the college student lounge. They are both very pleased to have found another person from their country with whom they can share their concerns. They often have quite animated discussion, in English, giving each other help and advice.

David, an American student usually sits nearby. One day, seemingly out of frustration, he asks, "Why do you two argue so much?" Ranjani and Sathie look at him in astonishment and do not know what to say.

How would you explain the situation? From the 18-theme culture-general framework, what issues might be operating here?

_____

_____

_____

_____

_____

_____

_____

_____

_____

_____

Of the following, what do you think is at the root of the problem?

1. David feels left out of the conversation and wishes the women would include him.
2. David is trying to work and is angry because the women are talking so much.
3. David is a rude person who should not be eavesdropping on other people's conversations.
4. David misinterprets the women's conversation as an argument when in fact it is a friendly discussion.

Feedback on these alternatives can be found on page 142

The Students Balk

Mrs. Allen teaches an elective class in English as a Standard Dialect. Her students (most of them African Americans, with some Latino students) have been identified by English teachers or guidance counselors as speaking an excessive amount of non-standard English. The students and their parents have chosen to take advantage of this special class.

Mrs. Allen's classroom is supplied with library carrels and tape recorders, along with the usual individual desks arranged in slightly cramped quarters at one end of the room. Mrs. Allen went to a great deal of effort to collect copies of written materials from a variety of sources and to make audiotapes for oral work. Each student took a placement test at the beginning of the year and received a binder full of individualized lessons geared to her or his particular needs.

On the days when the class stays together, working from a common textbook, the students concentrate and participate. Other days when they work individually, they complain, do not do much work, and some constantly visit others around the room. The only way Mrs. Allen can get individual work done is to act in a very authoritarian manner.

What would you do in this situation? From the 18-theme culture-general framework, what issues might be operating to explain the students' behavior?

_____

_____

_____

_____

_____

_____

_____

_____

Of the four alternatives below, what should the teacher know about the students that would help her to understand what is going on?

1. Kids, being human, are naturally lazy. If Mrs. Allen does not keep them together and under constant supervision, they will do the least amount of work possible.
2. Students from some cultural backgrounds value learning and doing in groups rather than learning from independent, individual efforts.
3. The students wanted attention from the teacher and discovered they could get it by being a "problem" for her.
4. The students resented studying this subject and expressed their resentment by not doing their work.

Feedback on these alternatives can be found on page 143

From a Fishing Village to a School in Town

Jimmie and his family had recently moved to Seattle from a small fishing village outside Anchorage where he had spent most of his young life among his father's people, the Tlingits. Jimmie often accompanied his father while he made his living fishing for salmon and hunting for the winter food supply.

Jimmie's mother taught him at home and he pursued his studies on his own with her guidance. When he came to Seattle he tested at grade level and was placed with other nine-year-olds in the fourth grade. In social studies, the class was broken into small groups, each having a different topic for group inquiry and presentation. Jimmie quietly sat at the edge of the group and did not share or discuss with them, even after several meetings, although he did seem to have his report outlined and completed. The group leader approached the teacher, complaining that Jimmie was not doing his fair share of the work.

Why do you think Jimmie was not doing his work? From the 18-theme culture-general framework, what issues might be operating to explain Jimmie's behavior?

_____

_____

_____

_____

_____

_____

_____

_____

_____

_____

Of the following, what is an appropriate explanation for Jimmie's quietness?

1. Jimmie is frightened of all the city children and is afraid to talk.
2. Jimmie doesn't like his new school and misses his home in Alaska.
3. Jimmie has always done his work on his own, and much of his learning has been on-the-job with his father.
4. Because Jimmie has not been in public school, he is really unable to do the work.

Feedback on these alternatives can be found on page 143

Careful Preparation of Lectures

Robert, an experienced agricultural engineering professor from New England, felt extremely fortunate to have been invited to spend four weeks in Texas, training four groups of young, English-speaking immigrant Mexican American farm workers. Each week he taught a different group in the use and maintenance of some new farm machinery that they were excited about using.

Robert spent hours in the instructional lab constructing diagrams explaining the use of the machines as well as maintenance of their parts. He was especially pleased with the diagrams he made that explained possible problems and actions one should take when a problem occurred. This media, combined with his extensive lecture notes, company operating manuals, films, books, and audio materials would assure the success of the program.

Much to his surprise, Robert found this teaching experience to be an extreme struggle both for himself and for his students. The first day seemed to go well, but the remaining four seemed long and drawn out. The students often complained about a lack of understanding. They were restless, talkative, and seemingly uninterested in what Robert had to offer. This really confused Robert as he had assumed that the students would be eager to learn the use of these machines that would ultimately improve crop yield.

What do you think is the source of the problem here? From the 18-theme cultural-general framework, what issues might explain the problem Robert is experiencing?

Of the following, which best explains the situation?

1. Robert's students were much younger than those he had initially been trained to teach.
2. Robert ignored the fact that most of his students speak Spanish (most commonly Tex-Mex) as well as English. He should have incorporated this into his presentation.
3. Migrant Mexican American farm workers are not accustomed to learning from books and papers. They often prefer to be taught with the real object.
4. The students resented Robert pushing his new technology on them and did not want this new machinery interfering with the methods to which they were accustomed.

Feedback on these alternatives can be found on page 144

The Chemistry Lab

Miguel, a 16-year-old Mexican student in Denver, has been in the U.S. for one year and can speak and understand English well enough to function in school. He has done well in his studies, carrying a 2.5 grade point average with his highest grades in literature and history courses. He struggled through the first semester of chemistry, however, with D's and F's on most tests, which were based on class lectures. His lab reports salvaged his grade because they were always of the highest quality — a fact that his teacher, Mr. Thompson, attributed mainly to the influence and help of Miguel's lab partner, Dave, the best student in the class.

When everyone was assigned a new lab partner for the second semester, Miguel was paired with Tim, who was failing the course. Miguel's lab reports, however, continued to be excellent, and Tim's also improved significantly. Mr. Thompson was puzzled by Miguel's performance.

How might Miguel's performance in chemistry class be explained? From the 18-theme cultural-general framework, what issues might be operating that help explain Miguel's performance?

_____

_____

_____

_____

_____

_____

_____

_____

_____

_____

Now, of the following, which best explains the situation?

1. Miguel does not listen attentively to the class lectures and does not, therefore, take adequate notes for the tests.
2. Miguel "freezes up" when taking tests.
3. Miguel learns better when he can discover things for himself and discuss his ideas with others. Thus, the lab environment is ideal for him.
4. Miguel lacks the analytic mind necessary to be successful in the study of science.
5. The lab sessions are less demanding than the material presented in class lectures.

Feedback on these alternatives can be found on page 144

Feedback on Critical Incidents

Rationales for: The Model Minority

1. You chose number 1. Hong Kong, where Wellington comes from, is a highly urbanized environment. The majority of Chinese from the People's Republic come from a very different, often a rural, setting. In addition, socioeconomic and class differences between Chinese from Hong Kong and Mainland China may also be at play. Mr. Fenwick has mistakenly put all Chinese into a single category, failing to make the finer distinctions necessary to more fully understand this group. This is the best response.

2. You chose number 2. We know that Mr. Fenwick has had extensive interaction with ethnic minorities in the school setting. There is a more appropriate response. Please choose again.

3. You chose number 3. Prior experience and expectations can often predispose one to expect certain behavior. In this case the text states that Mr. Fenwick did have certain prior experiences with Chinese that were quite different from those he is having with Wellington. It may very well be that Mr. Fenwick has unrealistic expectations of Wellington given his prior experience. This answer is partially correct.

4. You chose number 4. There is no indication in the story that Mr. Fenwick has taken a personal dislike to Wellington. Please select an explanation that reflects possible intercultural interaction.

Rationales for: The Proposal Process

1. You chose number 1. It is possible that Jose wanted to improve his proposal and get it adopted. He would have to leave the group he was working with to do this, however. Please choose another alternative.

2. You chose number 2. Jealousy is always a possible reaction when one person succeeds and another does not. However, among Filipinos this does not occur that often; it is probably not the main reason for Jose's request. In addition, since Stu's idea had been known previously by others in the group, Jose probably knew that it would be approved. Please choose another alternative.

3. You chose number 3. This is the best answer. Stu knows that in most American professional circles a person can be both a friend and a critic who makes constructive suggestions. This is true in most English-speaking countries. In fact, if Stu did not make constructive suggestions that in the long run would improve a friend's proposal, that friend could criticize

Stu for not helping him out. Among Filipinos, as well as many others from collectivist societies, the roles of friend and critic are differentiated, or separated. The same person cannot easily fill both roles. Thus, categorization as well as ingroup definitions are both operating here. Filipinos for the most part have set expectations about what a friend is, and Stu's behavior violated these expectations. It is possible that if Stu had made these suggestions in private Jose might not have felt so badly. Even then, however, Stu would want to be sure he was making suggestions in a style acceptable to Filipinos (and, in general, others from Southeast Asia). This preferred style would include saying a number of good things about a proposal, being much more indirect than he would with another American, and keeping the tone of the meeting light with jokes and anecdotes.

4. You chose number 4. While some might feel this, there is no indication that this is the case for Jose. Please select another alternative.

Rationales for Typical American Practice

1. While jealousy and resentment over grades are always possibilities, there is no evidence this is happening here. Please choose again.

2. Cultures differ in the amount of attention given to sojourners. Visitors to the United States frequently comment that Americans are polite during initial interaction but then seem indifferent at meeting the visitor a second or third time. For instance, foreign students may be introduced and made to feel welcome, but those same students seem to be forgotten a few days later. Keiko seems to be receiving this "typical" American treatment. It would help if Americans and all hosts tried to put themselves in the place of the newly-arrived person and then try to make him or her feel really at home, especially by including the person in social activities. In some respects, Keiko has been accepted and treated as she would be if she was another American. Keiko will have to work slowly to develop a more intimate, small ingroup where she is one-of-the-gang. This provides the best explanation.

3. This explanation has no basis in the narrative above. So far as we know, the faculty members were apparently sincere in their welcome and acted on their own initiative. Their behavior is the real problem, but their motives probably were not. Please choose again.

4. Most sojourners have some type of unrealistic expectation, and Keiko is probably no different. But she does not appear overly demanding of her

hosts. Her puzzlement and withdrawal seem well-founded and understandable. Look elsewhere for the real problem here.

Rationales for: *The Students Are Anxious, but Why?*

1. You chose number 1. There is a grain of truth to this. For some students who work slowly, strict time limits can be unnerving. In addition, people from some cultures do not have the same orientation to time as others may. However, there is more going on in this case. Please choose again.

2. You chose number 2. This is the best response for these circumstances. By the time these students reached high school they may have had many negative experiences with standardized tests, which tend to reflect white, middle-class culture and suburban school settings. Their expectations of failure may be quite high. While most probably could not verbalize the reasons for their reactions, they probably felt that they wouldn't do well and therefore may have tried to avoid the situation and/or relieve their tensions. This anxious behavior is what Ms. McConnell was seeing. If Ms. McConnell had been sensitive to the issue at hand, she would have directly addressed the students' anxiety about test taking. The fact that she did not, and that the students did not identify the cause of their uneasiness, was the direct cause of the students' undirected misbehavior. Teachers need to be sensitive to the anxieties of students who have regularly had the experience of receiving low grades and test scores.

3. You chose number 3. While this may be of concern to a few students, it does not realistically explain the generalized resistance Mary McConnell felt. Please choose again.

4. You chose number 4. On the contrary, students usually enjoy interruptions to the daily routine. They may not have enjoyed this particular type of interruption, however. There is a better alternative. Please select again.

Rationales for: *Saving Face*

1. You chose number 1. Here we have a typical case of an ambiguous situation. Teachers know (or think they know) the purpose of grades. Teachers also think they know what parents expect regarding the grading of students. Here, the teacher has assigned a grade that seems unacceptable to a parent. A decision is being forced on the principal. Neither party has complete knowledge or understanding of the system and assumptions under which the other lives.

Although this may seem like a challenge to Mrs. McMillen's judgment, this was the solution chosen to address this problem. The rationale for this action, as reported by the principal, was the father's emphasis on having his son achieve perfect grades and his desire to maintain the high "image" his family has attained. Having his son get an A in this and other courses is thus a "face-saving" issue for this Indian family, a common concern in many Eastern cultures. The principal, aware of the importance of this grade for the family's private and public image, justified discussing the situation with Mrs. McMillen to see if there was some way to change it, at least for this grading period. Presuming her ultimate agreement, this was determined to be the most sensitive way to deal with the situation. The father's request to have his son removed from the advanced-level class was his attempt to assure face-saving in the future – the son would simply do better in an easier class. The teacher and principal might then begin to help the family understand how the culture of an American school works, thus avoiding a similar situation in the future.

2. You chose number 2. This would probably not help the situation. In fact, to attack the father for his concern would be highly counter-productive. More attention should be given to the cause of the father's intense feelings about grades. Please choose again.

3. You chose number 3. This seems logical, but it will only reinforce the real basis of this problem. The student's father places a high premium on his son's grades because they reflect the worth of the entire family. Pointing out his son's math weaknesses will make the situation worse. Look elsewhere for an explanation of the cause and solution of this problem and try again.

4. You chose number 4. This could exacerbate an already touchy situation. The problem at this point is not with the student, but with the father. In addition, the cultural background of the family would probably not lend itself to this type of plan. The son is in no position to challenge his father or to persuade him to change his mind. Please choose again.

Rationales for: The Art Awards Ceremony

1. You chose number 1. Although Tony may have been overwhelmed at the attention and aware of Mr. Tarbell's position, there is really no indication that he was uncomfortable. Please choose again.

2. You chose number 2. Although Mr. Tarbell thought he was complimenting Tony, his use of language — specifically the phrase "uncanny ability to

paint"—implies a stereotyping of blacks as not artistic. To a white student, he might have said, "You are a very talented young artist,"—but Tony's ability to paint seems unnatural to him. Because of Mr. Tarbell's position Tony may have chosen to walk away rather than challenge him. You have selected the correct answer.

3. You chose number 3. His friends may have motioned him although there is no indication of this is the story. Choose another response.

4. You chose number 4. Although there may be something uncomfortable about the situation, nothing in the story really shows that Tony was embarrassed or uncomfortable. Choose another response.

Rationales for: The Missed Meeting

1. Mrs. Conant's concern seems sincere and well-founded, and the parents seem to appreciate it since they were immediately agreeable to the conference. The problem lies elsewhere. Please choose again.

2. Although the parents were obviously late for the appointment, there is no evidence to support the notion that they were intentionally insensitive or that they lacked concern for their daughter's progress. While "time" may be the main problem here, this attribution of motives and feelings is not justified by the evidence.

3. The differing views of "time" held by Mrs. Conant and the parents are the roots of the problem and the best explanations of the hurt feelings on both sides. The working unit of time for European Americans tends to be a five-minute block. Mrs. Conant, therefore, would probably consider that a person who is two or three minutes late for a meeting need not apologize. After five minutes, however, a short apology would be expected. Being 15 minutes late, representing three unit blocks of time, would require a lengthy, sincere apology, or perhaps a phone call in advance. Not all cultures, however, place the same emphasis on time and punctuality as do Western cultures. Historical perspectives are important to Arab people. The working unit of time for many Arabs (as well as for Latinos and Native Americans, among other people) is a much longer block than it is for Westerners. Mrs. Conant and the parents are, therefore, victims of conflicting views of time and punctuality. This is the best response.

4. All the evidence suggests that Mrs. Conant is most agreeable to have conferences during her free period. Indeed, she initiates this meeting. Please choose again.

Rationales for: Bad Calls on the Tennis Court

1. While this alternative may have some validity, it does not get at the underlying cause of Pitchit's behavior. Please choose again.

2. Pitchit's successful 7-1 record indicates that he does have impressive talent as a tennis player. There is no evidence that he feels at all inferior. Please choose again.

3. If Coach Butler had watched the entire match, Pitchit may not have been a victim of bad calls. This, however, has nothing to do with his passive reaction in this situation. Please make another choice.

4. This is the best response. In Thai and many other Asian cultures, assertiveness is not highly valued; it is often seen as a potentially disruptive trait. Socialization in such cultures encourages a certain degree of passivity; a willingness to tolerate unpleasant situations without complaint to a much greater degree than is manifested in Western cultures. Such passivity has its roots in both the religious (Buddhist) and environmental forces that have shaped Asian culture. Pitchit, therefore, is hesitant to assert himself against his opponent, even though he knows he is being cheated.

Rationales for: What Happened to Mariko?

1. It seems that Mariko did have ample opportunity to explain to Mr. Simms why she could not or would not work at the fair. There is no evidence that she was really "railroaded" into this. Look elsewhere for the deeper reason for her hesitancy to tell Mr. Simms why she wouldn't attend.

2. This is the best response. Many cultures consider it rude to communicate a direct rejection or refusal. Hesitancy and ambiguity are used to convey reluctance and to avoid embarrassment to either party. Mr. Simms and Julie are undoubtedly puzzled by Mariko's lack of forthrightness. To Mariko, however, honesty is of lesser value than preserving dignity in interpersonal interactions, and one of the main sources of cultural conflict in this situation is the differing weights attached to honesty. While many Western cultures view the direct and honest statement of intentions or opinions as a positive trait, others regard such behavior as discourteous.

3. While this face-saving motive has some plausibility, Mariko's hesitant reaction seems to have a different cause. There is no evidence here that Mariko's pride has been wounded or that she is in any way angry with Mr. Simms or Julie. Please choose again.

4. Mariko shows no resentment at being asked to do something outside of school time. Look elsewhere for an explanation of her hesitancy and evasiveness.

Rationales for: Conversation at Lunch

1. You selected number 1. There is nothing in the incident to indicate that David wants to be included in the conversation. Please select another response.
2. You selected number 2. Although this is possible, David would probably not try to do his work in the lounge if he knew that these women were always in there at this time. Please select another response.
3. You selected number 3. There is nothing in the incident to indicate that David is rude. The conversation was quite loud. Please select another response.
4. You selected number 4. This is the best choice. Indian women rather frequently have animated conversations in which they interrupt one another and give unsolicited advice. In David's experience, discussions with this tone, especially between women, were arguments. David has misinterpreted this style of communication.

Rationales for: The Students Balk

1. You have chosen number 1. While there may be some truth to this response, depending on what teaching style the students are familiar with, it is not a valid maxim to teach by. In general, students, when motivated, can work well on their own. Please choose again.
2. You have chosen number 2. This is the most appropriate answer. The teacher was expecting that these students would enjoy working on their own. She did not realize that her students were from a background that tends to have a group orientation and values joint work. Her students were far more comfortable not being singled out for individual programmed study.
3. You have chosen number 3. As many teachers know, this motivation is sometimes behind "trouble-makers" in the classroom. However as the behavior is widespread in the classroom, there seems to be something else going on. Please choose again.
4. You have chosen number 4. Teaching English as a Standard Dialect at the high school level is quite unusual, and the issues involved can be volatile. For these reasons it is quite plausible that students may resent studying

this subject. However, the students seemed to work well when they worked as a whole class. In addition, this class is an elective and there are no clues given that lead one to that conclusion in this case. Please choose again.

Rationales for: *From a Fishing Village to a School in Town*

1. You chose number 1. There is no indication that this is his reaction. Jimmie may be unfamiliar with the setting of the city and new children, but there is a more comprehensive response. Please choose again.
2. You chose number 2. Though Jimmie may miss his home and may not be comfortable at the new school, this is not clear and does not explain Jimmie's behavior with the inquiry groups. Please consider again.
3. You chose number 3. Jimmie has learned primarily by studying on his own and by practical application of skills in working and living. He has developed strong independent study skills and is not used to group involvement. Jimmie may need further guidance in adapting to group study. Perhaps he could begin by working with a partner, then move to small groups before working on a larger group project. He should also be encouraged to continue his independent work and may have much to offer the others in this area. This is the best response.
4. You chose number 4. As Jimmie tested at grade level successfully, he is clearly able to do the work. Choose again.

Rationales for: *Careful Preparation of Lectures*

1. You chose alternative 1. Although there is an increasing body of knowledge and literature emerging that focuses on the adult learner and that should be utilized when planning instruction for adults, the students in this incident were not that much older than the students Robert was accustomed to teaching. These young farm workers would not require these kinds of modifications. Please select another response.
2. You chose alternative 2. Although these workers probably all speak Spanish, they also understand and regularly speak Standard English. This is not a critical factor here. Please select another alternative.
3. You chose alternative 3. It has been found that many Mexican American farm workers (as well as many other people from cultures without a long experience with a written language) typically teach each other and, therefore, learn in-context rather than out-of-context. While Robert's professional training and experiences have stressed out-of-context learning of

material (through books, films, lectures, and so forth), which would be applied at a later time, many people learn more and become more involved and motivated when taught in an in-context situation. An out-of-classroom, hands-on approach would probably facilitate their learning process. This is the best response.

4. You chose alternative 4. There is no indication that the workers resented Robert or the fact that he was introducing new machinery. In fact, the incident mentions that the workers were looking forward to using these machines. Please choose again.

Rationales for: The Chemistry Lab

1. There is no evidence that Miguel does not pay attention or that he fails to take adequate notes. Please choose again.
2. Since Miguel has a 2.5 grade point average, he must be doing well in tests in some of his courses. Freezing up on tests is, therefore, probably not the reason for his performance in chemistry class.
3. Since Miguel does consistently well in lab work, he probably feels more comfortable and confident in such a "hands-on," "shared-responsibility" learning situation. The emphasis of lab work on activity, exploration, and group learning matches the learning style of Miguel's cultural background. This is the best answer.
4. Miguel's performance in lab work shows that he does have the analytic ability necessary to understand scientific concepts. This is not an adequate explanation for his performance. Please choose again.
5. No evidence indicates that the lab sessions are less demanding. Please choose another response.

Observing Cultural Differences

Purpose

To apply the 18-theme culture-general framework to casual observations made during interactions with others.

Instructions

Make extended observations of yourself as well as others over the course of about a week. The focus of your observations should be on potential misunderstanding or miscommunication between people of different cultural backgrounds (remember that we define cultural rather broadly). Record your observations as precisely as possible, identifying any and all of the culture-general themes that you believe apply. Finally, propose alternative explanations or attributions for the behavior you have observed from two (or more) perspectives. Use the following as a guide, but do not necessarily limit yourself to the space provided. You should make *at least* ten different relevant observations. Make additional copies of this form if needed.

Interaction as I Observed It	*Cultural-General Theme(s)*	*Possible Attributions*
Example: Two girls, one Mexican, the other Canadian European discuss plans of what they will do Friday night. Mexican girl insists upon asking her parents' permission before making commitment to Canadian friend.	Family roles Individualism vs collectivism	Collectivist orientation (tendency for Mexicans). May require approval from others before taking action, whereas Canadian (individualistic tendency) is more comfortable making her own plans.

Interaction as I Observed It	Cultural-General Theme(s)	Possible Attributions

Interaction as I Observed It	Cultural-General Theme(s)	Possible Attributions

Activity 18

Learning about Others

Purpose

To learn about culture differences by interviewing someone from a different cultural or ethnic group while applying concepts from the culture-general framework.

Instructions

Find someone from a culture different from your own to interview (preferably someone outside your immediate and known peer group). Try to choose someone you think will have different attitudes, opinions, and experiences from yourself. Choose some questions from the list that follows, or develop some of your own. Before you interview the person, answer these questions for yourself. For each of the questions, follow up with "Why?" in order to explore underlying values. Take notes of the responses. Discuss the questions and the "why" with the other person until you have found at least five major areas where there are clear differences between your answer and the other person's. Also be sure to identify five major areas where you are in agreement with one another. Prepare a short paper or presentation that summarizes your findings.

a. Whom should you obey? Why?

b. Who makes decisions (at home, school, community)? Why?

c. How should you behave with others (elders, children, neighbors)? Why?

d. Whom should you respect? How do you show respect? Why?

e. How should you act in public so you bring credit or honor to your family? Why?

f. What does it mean to be successful in life? Why?

g. Whom should you trust? Why?

h. What are the signs of success? Why?

i. What provides "security" in life? Why?

j. Who should your friends be? Who decides? Why?

k. Where, and with whom, should you live? Why?

l. Whom should you marry? At about what age? Who decides? Why?

m. What is expected of children when they are young? Why?

n. What should you depend on others for? Why?

o. When should you be self-sufficient, if ever? Why?

p. What should you expose to others, and what should be kept private? Why?

q. How should you plan for your future? Why?

r. What should be remembered from your heritage? Why?

s. What was better when you were younger or during your parents' youth? Why?

t. What do you wish for your children that you could not have? Why?

What did you learn about the other person that is significantly different from you? How might this knowledge affect the interviewee as a learner? You as a teacher?

_____

_____

_____

_____

_____

_____

_____

_____

_____

_____

_____

_____

_____

_____

_____

_____

Community Scan: Analyzing Available Resources that Support Multicultural Education

Purpose

To develop a deeper understanding of a local community in terms of resources available that support as well as hinder the goals and objectives of multicultural education.

Instructions

Select a community available that you can study on a firsthand basis using the following as a guideline. Plan to survey a community over a period of a few days by studying a small section or neighborhood at a time. You may do this activity individually, but it is better if this can be accomplished in small groups. If done in small groups, each group should take responsibility for a different neighborhood, but be certain to select neighborhoods that all serve a common school. Later, share your findings with others so all may gain a more complete understanding of the area, what influences children are exposed to, and what resources might be available to educators.

1. Before you begin your observation, make a list of the things you expect to find that support multicultural education as well as those that pose threats or obstacles.

   _____

   _____

   _____

   _____

   _____

   _____

   _____

   _____

2. Begin by walking the area you are to analyze. What resources do you find that may support efforts to increase understanding of diversity and multicultural education? For instance, what ethnic groups are present? What languages are spoken? What global links are evident? What places of worship exist? What ethnic restaurants and ethnic food stores can be found? What community services exist to assist the poor, the elderly, or the disabled?

_____

_____

_____

_____

_____

_____

_____

_____

_____

_____

3. Interview storeowners and shopkeepers in the neighborhood. What are their impressions of the cultural diversity in the community? How is diversity an asset or an obstacle to them? What is their impression of the role schools play in addressing issues of diversity?

_____

_____

_____

_____

_____

_____

_____

_____

_____

4. What community resources or industries can you identify that may offer possible school-community linkages or other ways to relate curriculum to the community and the environment?

_____

_____

_____

_____

_____

_____

5. What unique cultural experiences and resources do you think children will bring with them to school as a result of growing up in this community? How might you build upon these in the classroom and school? You might benefit by drawing a community map of your findings.

_____

_____

_____

_____

_____

_____

6. What unique aspects of this community do you think might hinder a school's ability to effectively address multicultural or diversity education? How might you overcome these?

_____

_____

_____

_____

_____

7. What aspects of community life do you still have questions about? How might you go about finding the answers to these?

_____

_____

_____

_____

_____

_____

_____

_____

_____

8. Describe any surprises, unexpected outcomes, or concerns of your community scan.

_____

_____

_____

_____

_____

_____

_____

_____

_____

Examining Stereotypes Held By Self and Others

(Adapted from Ponterotto and Pedersen, 1993)

Purpose

To identify, describe and evaluate "frequently expressed" stereotypes about different groups of people.

Instructions

Identify up to five different groups to consider. Then, complete the checklist for the agreed-upon groups by placing a check mark alongside the adjectives that are representative of that group. Compare your patterns of similarity and difference with peers in small groups.

Group A = _____   Group B = _____

Group C = _____   Group D = _____

Group E = _____

Adjectives	Group A	Group B	Group C	Group D	Group E
Not at all aggressive					
Conceited about appearance					
Very ambitious					
Very independent					
Always acting as leaders					
Does not hide emotions					

Adjectives	Group A	Group B	Group C	Group D	Group E
Very active					
Very logical					
Not at all competitive					
Feelings easily hurt					
Strong need for security					
Self-confident					
Has difficulty making decisions					
Very passive					
Very direct					
Very adventurous					
Hard-working and industrious					
Very submissive					
Easy going					
Knows the ways of the world					

Working in small groups, compare patterns of similarity and difference of stereotypes believed to be held about each group. Because there tends to be much emotion surrounding stereotypes, it is not necessary to indicate whether or not you agree with the stereotype – just that you identify it as one you believe to be common about the group.

How did you feel while completing this activity?

_____

_____

_____

_____

_____

_____

_____

How did actual group members of any of the racial, cultural or ethnic groups mentioned respond to the results as well as the subsequent discussion?

_____

_____

_____

_____

_____

_____

_____

_____

What have you learned about the use of stereotypes?

_____

_____

_____

_____

_____

_____

_____

_____

Stereotypes and their Impact on Interaction and Learning

Purpose

To recognize stereotypes of various groups and how they affect interaction and learning.

Instructions

Stereotypes refer to a belief about the personal attributes of individuals based on the inaccurate generalizations used to describe all members of a group, thus ignoring individual differences. Try to identify at least three stereotypes of each group identified below, state the source of these stereotypes, and explain how they affect interaction and learning.

Group	Example of the stereotype	Its source	How it affects interaction and learning
Lesbians and gay men	all homosexuals are interested in me as a sexual object.	friends	fear of interaction

Group	Example of the stereotype	Its source	How it affects interaction and learning
Latinos/ Hispanics	Latino men are all macho	movies/TV	fear that female child (or my student) will be treated as a second class citizen

Group	Example of the stereotype	Its source	How it affects interaction and learning
Asian	Asian women are submissive	movies/TV	may not be offered positions of power and authority

Continue in this manner, identifying a group, generating a list of stereotypes, and analyzing their impact on interaction and learning. You might include such groups as African Americans, European Americans, Catholics, teenagers, the elderly, and so forth.

Group	Example of the stereotype	Its source	How it affects interaction and learning

Reflection

1. What have been the major sources of the stereotypes?

   _____

   _____

   _____

   _____

   _____

2. In what ways have stereotypes affected intercultural interaction?

   _____

   _____

   _____

   _____

   _____

   _____

   _____

   _____

3. In what ways might stereotypes affect learning?

   _____

   _____

   _____

   _____

   _____

   _____

   _____

   _____

   _____

   _____

4. What might teachers do to help reduce the likelihood that students will use stereotypes?

_____

_____

_____

_____

_____

_____

_____

_____

_____

_____

_____

_____

_____

_____

_____

_____

_____

_____

_____

_____

_____

_____

_____

_____

_____

_____

How to Respond Stereotypes

(Adapted from Goldstein, 2000)

Purpose

To develop strategies and skill in responding to stereotypic statements.

Instructions

Review the various strategies described below. Then read the scenario that follows and respond to the corresponding questions.

1. Propose alternative attributions or explanations for someone's behavior.

   Stereotype: Those international exchange students think they are better than anyone else; they only associate with each other.

   Response: If I were from another country I might feel more comfortable with other people who shared a similar experience. Maybe we should try to get to know them, and after they are here a while they will have other friends.

* * * * *

2. Help others see that people who tend to be more visible my not be typical.

   Stereotype: There's Joe, the head of the Gay Student Association. Those people sure look outrageous.

   Response: His appearance may be rather unusual, but most gay and lesbian students look no different from anyone else.

* * * * *

3. Be a cultural interpreter

   Stereotype: What is it with those people? I try to be nice and talk to them but they're always rude and getting in my face.

   Response: I think Roberto and Ricardo are also trying to be nice. In Mexican culture, it is common to stand closer to another person than we typically do.

* * * * *

4. Point out within-group differences

   Stereotype: I'm tired of working with the special needs students. They are so helpless and needy.

   Response: Well, maybe Susan does require a lot of attention because of her disability, but James and Amanda are more independent and can interact with others in different ways.

* * * * *

5. Point out similarities across groups.

   Stereotype: Those people are so loud.

   Response: Sometimes people get carried away when they're having fun or having a party. Did you hear all the noise coming from our fraternity last night?

* * * * *

6. Indicate when conclusions are based on limited experience.

   Stereotype: You have to watch those Arabs closely. They could be terrorists.

   Response: That sounds like you're referring to certain Arabs you've seen on television. I don't think I've ever really met an Arab, have you?

* * * * *

7. Point out information that does not support the stereotype.

   Stereotype: All Asians are smart. Lisa only gets A's on everything she does.

   Response: Perhaps, but she does seem to study all the time.

* * * * *

Scenario: Two high school seniors are waiting for a new student who will join their sport team. They have just learned that he is African American. They are not African American.

Stereotype: Did you hear our new teammate is Black? Wow, it must be something to have grown up in the ghetto.

Response: (Hint: Point out information that does not support the stereotype.)

_____

_____

Stereotype: There was one Black guy that went to my other school and he was an amazing athlete.

Response: (Hint: Explain that individuals who are more visible may be atypical and/or you may point out within-group differences)

_____

_____

Stereotype: He didn't show up for the first team meeting. He must not be very serious.

Response: (Hint: Point out alternative explanations, or point out information that does not support the stereotype.)

_____

_____

Stereotype: I just hope that all of us can get along. It could be tough, you know.

Response: (Hint: Point out similarities across groups.)

_____

_____

On a separate paper, create your own scenario, a set of plausible stereotypes, as well as alternative responses.

Privilege: The Invisible Knapsack

(adapted from Summerfield, 1997)

Purpose

To explore institutional biases, the oftentimes unexamined privileges held by members of certain groups, typically able-bodied, heterosexual, European Americans, that enables them to move with relative ease throughout society.

Instructions

In her paper, *White Privilege and Male Privilege*, Peggy McIntosh (1988) uses racism as a way to demonstrate the nature and depth of institutional bias people typically take for granted in society. Explore the benefits certain groups have in society by responding to the following questions.

1. Begin by thinking about some of the benefits you think white people have in society and take for granted that non-whites may not have. Before reviewing McIntosh's list, try to identify at least five privileges you think would be included on the list:

   _____

   _____

   _____

   _____

   _____

2. Now, compare your results with some of the following from McIntosh's original list. McIntosh identified such privileges of Whites as:

   - When they go into stores, they won't automatically be viewed as potential shoplifters.
   - When they go to college, they won't automatically be thought of in terms of "affirmative action" admits (or "affirmative action" hires if this is a workplace).

- When they apply for a bank loan, they won't automatically be viewed as a bad credit risk.
- When they attend school or begin a new job, they will find role models of similar background.
- When they apply for a job, the people in power will be of their race.
- When they speak up in a group, they will not be assumed to be speaking on behalf of an entire community, but of themselves.
- When they study history in school, they will learn about their own heritage.
- When they walk down a street at night they will not be perceived as a threat.

Now that you have read some of McIntosh's original list, can you think of any other privileges that may exist for whites in society?

_____

_____

_____

_____

_____

3. The same exercise can be completed to examine institutional biases against many groups in society, such as the elderly, gays and lesbians, the disabled, or the poor. It may be easier to generate a list if you are a member of a particular group however this is not always the case. In some instances, people may attribute difficulties or barriers to their own shortcomings or lack of ability, and they may be invisible even to themselves.

Now, identify another group in society and generate at least five examples of 'invisible' barriers that may confront its members.

Group: _____

_____

_____

_____

_____

_____

4. Many people who enjoy privileges fail to recognize them. While they may understand that slavery and a lack of voting rights for African Americans and women are forms of institutional discrimination, they may falsely assume that since these wrongs have been corrected society as a whole is fair and equal. A beginning step at dismantling institutional discrimination is to do your own consciousness-raising. If you are one that is discriminated against, it is important to gain as much clarity of the situation as possible. If you are a beneficiary of the system, you should begin to examine ways in which you can change things.

   What are some things that you can do, both personally and professionally, to address such issues?

   _____

   _____

   _____

   _____

   _____

   _____

   _____

   _____

   _____

Institutional Discrimination

*(Adapted from
Goldstein, 2000)*

Purpose

To distinguish between individual and institutional discrimination and practices that perpetuate racism.

Instructions

Institutional discrimination refers to policies and practices of institutions that allow racism to persist, along with other forms of inequity. Below, you will be presented with a number of situations. You will be asked to determine if these policies or practices systematically privilege members of certain groups while discriminating against members of other groups. Complete the three questions that follow for each of the following that you determine to be an example of institutional discrimination.

1. Children of teachers employed in this private school receive free tuition.

   Is this an example of discrimination?   _____ Yes   _____ No

   a. Against which groups, if any, might this policy discriminate?

   _____

   _____

   _____

   b. What is the purpose of the policy?

   _____

   _____

   _____

c. If the purpose is valid, how else might it be achieved?

_____

_____

_____

2. A public meeting about the future of the schools is held on the third floor of a building that does not have elevators.

   Is this an example of discrimination?   _____ Yes   _____ No

   a. Against which groups, if any, might this policy discriminate?

   _____

   _____

   _____

   b. What is the purpose of the policy?

   _____

   _____

   _____

   c. If the purpose is valid, how else might it be achieved?

   _____

   _____

   _____

3. A school system decides to fill a vacant position "in-house" rather than advertise.

   Is this an example of discrimination?   _____ Yes   _____ No

   a. Against which groups, if any, might this policy discriminate?

   _____

   _____

   _____

b. What is the purpose of the policy?

_____

_____

_____

c. If the purpose is valid, how else might it be achieved?

_____

_____

_____

4. A local religious school offers reduced tuition for members of its faith.

Is this an example of discrimination?   _____ Yes   _____ No

a. Against which groups, if any, might this policy discriminate?

_____

_____

_____

b. What is the purpose of the policy?

_____

_____

_____

c. If the purpose is valid, how else might it be achieved?

_____

_____

_____

5. Because a recent school levy failed, a new school policy states that children who wish to participate in sports or musical performing groups must pay for their own uniforms.

   Is this an example of discrimination?   _____ Yes   _____ No

   a. Against which groups, if any, might this policy discriminate?

   _____

   _____

   _____

   b. What is the purpose of the policy?

   _____

   _____

   _____

   c. If the purpose is valid, how else might it be achieved?

   _____

   _____

   _____

6. A teacher awards ten points (out of 100 for the total assignment) to boys who wear a jacket and tie and girls who wear a full-length dress during an oral presentation as part of the final grade in a business speech class.

   Is this an example of discrimination?   _____ Yes   _____ No

   a. Against which groups, if any, might this policy discriminate?

   _____

   _____

   _____

   b. What is the purpose of the policy?

   _____

   _____

   _____

c. If the purpose is valid, how else might it be achieved?

_____

_____

_____

7. The local fire department requires that all applicants for firefighting positions be at least 5'6" tall.

   Is this an example of discrimination?   _____ Yes   _____ No

   a. Against which groups, if any, might this policy discriminate?

   _____

   _____

   _____

   b. What is the purpose of the policy?

   _____

   _____

   _____

   c. If the purpose is valid, how else might it be achieved?

   _____

   _____

   _____

Biracial Identity and the Classroom

(Adapted from Goldstein, 2000)

Purpose

To explore the influence of biracial identity development in children.

Instructions

Our nation has witnessed a steady increase in the number of children born of parents of different ethnic or racial background; a rate that has tripled in the past 20 years. Observation of biracial individuals has concluded the following (Root, 1998):

- Racial or ethnic appearance does not necessarily predict racial or ethnic identity.
- Individuals of mixed race/ethnicity are increasingly likely to identify themselves as racially or ethnically mixed.
- An individual's racial or ethnic identity may change over time and across situations.
- Siblings of the same mixed heritage may have different racial or ethnic identities.

Respond to each of the questions below in the space provided.

1. Imagine that you are the child of an African American father and a European American mother. Describe your likely racial identity. Why did you choose the particular identity?

_____

_____

_____

_____

_____

2. Describe how this racial/ethnic identity might change under the following conditions:

   a. You live only with your mother.

   _____

   _____

   _____

   b. You live only with your father.

   _____

   _____

   _____

   c. You have the appearance of a White person.

   _____

   _____

   _____

   d. You have the appearance of a Black person.

   _____

   _____

   _____

   e. Your appearance is racially ambiguous.

   _____

   _____

   _____

   f. You live in a predominantly Black neighborhood.

   _____

   _____

   _____

g. You live in a predominantly White neighborhood.

_____

_____

_____

h. You live in a racially-mixed neighborhood and have friends from many different ethnic groups.

_____

_____

_____

i. If you live with your mother only, she discourages you from exploring the identity of your father.

_____

_____

_____

j. If you live with your father only, he discourages you from exploring the identity of your mother.

_____

_____

_____

k. Your parents rarely discuss race or ethnicity.

_____

_____

_____

l. Your family has experienced discrimination in the neighborhood.

_____

_____

_____

m. You have experienced discrimination in school.

_____

_____

_____

n. You are male.

_____

_____

_____

o. You are female.

_____

_____

_____

3. Which of the factors identified above are the most important to you? The least?

_____

_____

_____

_____

4. What other factors or experiences might a biracial child encounter that were not identified above?

_____

_____

_____

_____

_____

_____

_____

_____

Interviewing Non-Native English Speakers About Their Experiences in this Country

Purpose

To raise awareness and sensitivity, and learn about the problems faced by new immigrants, international students or new speakers of English.

Instructions

Interview a person who first came to the United States speaking limited or no English. This person might be an international student on campus, or a student and/or parent who came to the United States speaking minimal English (feel free to adjust the questions accordingly to accommodate the person you are interviewing).

1. Describe some of the initial difficulties or problems you encountered when you first arrived in this country. To what would you attribute the problems?

   _____

   _____

   _____

   _____

   _____

2. What significant cultural differences did you encounter in the early stages of your adjustment to this country? How did you overcome these?

   _____

   _____

   _____

   _____

   _____

3. What primary language did you speak before coming to the United States? Describe your competency as a speaker of your home language. Then, describe your competency as a speaker of English.

_____

_____

_____

_____

4. What communication problems did you experience when you first came to this country? How did you handle these?

_____

_____

_____

_____

_____

_____

5. What kinds of communication difficulties, if any, do you currently face?

_____

_____

_____

_____

_____

_____

6. What might people (or schools and/or teachers if interviewing a child or parent) in the United States do that would help to reduce adjustment and communication difficulties for new immigrants?

_____

_____

_____

_____

_____

7. What messages do you have for other non-English speakers that might make their adjustment and communication easier?

_____

_____

_____

_____

_____

_____

_____

In conclusion: What can you conclude about communication, culture shock and adjustment that would be useful for teachers?

_____

_____

_____

_____

_____

_____

_____

_____

_____

_____

_____

What Does It Feel Like to Be Excluded?

Purpose

To develop empathy by imagining what it might be like to be excluded or discriminated against, and to propose possible responses.

Instructions

Developing an understanding of the experience of others in a pluralistic society is critical if teachers and students are to develop a fuller knowledge of culture and its various forms. One way to develop such a skill is to listen to the voices of individuals who have felt excluded from the mainstream for one reason or another—perhaps due to outright, overt racism; subtle, institutional racism; general ignorance; subtle pressure; or genuine dislike. Read the following quotes and try to identify one or two feelings associated with them. Then, consider what you as a teacher might say and do in response (adapted from an exercise developed by Beth Swadener).

Low-income mother: "My son understands that we have no money the last week of each month, and yet he was pressured by his teacher to have a new workbook by the next class. When we could not afford it that week he was made to sit out of class. The teacher said, "Everyone else remembered to get their book, why not you?"

As the mother, I feel

_____

_____

_____

As a teacher, I might

_____

_____

_____

Jewish parent: "Last year our daughter asked me, 'Could we have a Christmas tree and just not use it?'"

As the parent, I feel

_____

_____

_____

As a teacher, I might

_____

_____

_____

Chinese parent: "My daughter asked me, 'Can I have blonde hair? It's better to be blonde, Dad!'"

As the parent, I feel

_____

_____

_____

As a teacher, I might

_____

_____

_____

Native American father: "The schools continue to miseducate my son. The images he has of native people are limited, and there is virtually no relevant Native American history taught in his school."

As the father, I feel

_____

_____

_____

As a teacher, I might

_____

_____

_____

Islamic parent: "My child's school has many Christian-based activities and has never even recognized that some of the students are not Christian."

As the parent, I feel

_____

_____

_____

As a teacher, I might

_____

_____

_____

Single parent mother: "I feel that all my son's behavior at school is blamed on the fact that I'm a single parent, and that many judgments about our family are made based on no other evidence than our 'single parent family' status."

As the mother, I feel

_____

_____

_____

As a teacher, I might

_____

_____

_____

Vietnamese parent: (translated from Vietnamese) "My children speak and read better English than I do. It is so hard when lots of letters and information come home from school in English. I also feel that my children are losing respect for their parents and the elders in this country."

As the parent, I feel

_____

_____

_____

As a teacher, I might

_____

_____

_____

Extend this activity by collecting some of your own quotes from statements by children, parents, and other community members that represent diverse groups and who have felt excluded. Record three examples below.

_____

_____

_____

_____

_____

_____

_____

_____

_____

_____

_____

_____

Gender Role Socialization

Purpose

To identify some of the ways males and females are differentially socialized in mainstream American society.

Instructions

The following are generalizations concerning gender role socialization in American society. Provide an example of each, either from your own experience or from what you have witnessed in society in general. Then respond to the reflective questions.

A Woman is Taught	My Example	A Man is Taught	My Example
To do what she is asked	_____	To control	_____
To be pleasing to a man	_____	To score, to achieve	_____
To hurt no one's feelings	_____	To pursue goals, to take charge	_____
To look good	_____	To discuss women's bodies	_____
To be taken care of	_____	To have a dream	_____
To compete for male attention	_____	To work as a team	_____
To care for others before self	_____	To take risks and challenges	_____
To follow rules	_____	To make rules and decisions	_____
To let others make choices	_____	To put women on a pedestal	_____
To be friendly, helpful	_____	To expect service from women	_____

Which of these are advantages in American society?

_____

_____

_____

_____

_____

_____

Which of these are disadvantages in American society?

_____

_____

_____

_____

_____

_____

How are some of these perpetuated in schools?

_____

_____

_____

_____

_____

_____

Observing Gender Differences

Purpose

To develop a deeper understanding of the influence gender plays in development, socialization, and in education.

Instructions

Read the following story, which you may have already heard. Then, do the following activities and respond to the reflective questions that follow.

A father and his son were in a terrible automobile accident. They were injured so severely that they were taken to different hospitals. The son required immediate surgery, so a surgeon was called in. The surgeon walked into the operating room, took one look at the patient, and said, "I can't operate on this boy. This boy is my son!" How can this be?

It should be obvious to you that the surgeon was the boy's mother. For the most part, when we think of surgeons, or doctors in general, most of us do not expect them to be women. Although much has been written and done in recent years to change the way people think about gender and the various roles people adopt, peoples' thinking along these lines tends to be rather static. Far too many people still think of men as managers, administrators, and leaders and women as subordinates, holding other stereotypic roles (e.g. secretaries, nurses, and oftentimes teachers).

The following activities will help you to gain a deeper picture of the influence gender plays in development, socialization, and in education.

A. Arrange to do observations of children's play behavior at a nearby school, both of preschool and elementary children. Summarize your observations by responding to the following questions.

When observing preschool boys and girls, what gender differences are you able to observe? Think of the way children act, their choices of play activities as well as playmates, and their responses to various stimuli.

_____

_____

_____

_____

_____

Do a similar comparison of elementary-aged children (you may wish to restrict this to specific age groups, such as seven- and eight-year-olds, nine- and ten-year-olds, etc.). What do you notice?

_____

_____

_____

_____

_____

_____

What happens when you ask boys and girls to play with a toy or game typically assigned to the other sex?

_____

_____

_____

_____

_____

_____

B. Using a week's worth of your campus or local newspaper, circle every headline in which females or males are mentioned. Compare the number of mentions of each. Compare the number of roles associated with males and females (e.g., husband, wife, banker, politician, daughter, son athlete, etc.). In what sections of the paper are males and females referred to most often? Is there a difference between the campus newspaper, the local paper, a national paper? What generalizations are you able to make given your observations?

_____

_____

_____

_____

_____

_____

_____

_____

C. Examine the textbooks used in teacher education and arts and sciences. Look for evidence of gender bias discussed or presented in various chapters. One interesting activity is to count and compare the number of males and females listed in the index. Do the same for various textbooks used in elementary and secondary schools. What generalizations are you able to make given your observations?

_____

_____

_____

_____

_____

_____

_____

_____

D. Make a comparison of the chores you were expected to do at home as you were growing up. If you have brothers or sisters, were their chores similar or different? If you were an only child, or had only siblings of the same sex, talk to someone else who had siblings of the opposite sex. How were your chores similar or different? What does this suggest?

_____

_____

_____

_____

_____

_____

_____

_____

E. Do a comparison study among your classmates in terms of the number and kinds of math and science courses each took in high school. Is there any difference between the males and the females? Can people describe the reasons for taking or not taking math and science courses? Compare reasons of males versus females. What generalizations are you able to make given your observations?

_____

_____

_____

_____

_____

_____

_____

_____

The Plight of Women on a Global Scale

Purpose

To become better informed about the experience of women on a global scale and to project oneself into the experience of the other.

Instructions

Read and respond to the following.

The majority of the information we have about people in the world (including most of the social and behavioral science research) has been based on the experience of males, or is presented in gender-neutral language (although it still may be based on the experience of males. See Carol Gilligan's book, *In A Different Voice*, to understand how the experience of females is oftentimes quite different than that of males and from that reported in much of the research literature). Following is some information about women in the world that you might consider (adapted from Drum, Hughes and Otero, 1994):

a. While women make up more than half of the world's population, they do two-thirds of the world's work, both paid and unpaid, and receive only one-tenth of the world's wages.
b. Rural women account for more than half of the food produced in the developing world, and for as much as 80 percent of the food production in Africa.
c. The hourly wages of working women in the manufacturing industry are on average three-fourths those earned by men.
d. In the United States, on the average, women earn 70 percent of each dollar earned by men.
e. In 1950, there were 27 million more boys than girls enrolled in schools worldwide. Currently there are 80 million more boys than girls enrolled in schools.
f. Nutritional anemia afflicts half of all women of childbearing age in developing countries, compared with less than 7 percent of women of childbearing age in developed countries.

g. In the developing world, two-thirds of the women over the age of 25 (and about one-half the men) have never been to school.

h. Ten of the eleven oldest democracies in the world did not grant women the right to vote until the 20th century. The first to establish electoral equality was New Zealand in 1893. The last to establish electoral equality was Switzerland in 1971.

i. Women represent 50 percent of the voting population in the world but hold only 10 percent of the seats in national legislatures.

What do you think about and feel when you read these statistics?

_____

_____

_____

_____

If you could choose to be any gender, which would you choose to be and why?

_____

_____

_____

_____

Which gender would you choose if you lived in the Third World and why?

_____

_____

_____

_____

When do either women or men encounter injustice as a result of their gender?

_____

_____

_____

_____

If you could choose a gender for your child, which would you choose, and why?

_____

_____

_____

_____

Now, imagine you are of the opposite gender. How might your answers to these questions be different?

_____

_____

_____

_____

_____

_____

_____

_____

Sexual Orientation: A Matter of Experience?

Purpose

To examine potential classroom situations that reflect others as well as your own responses to issues surrounding sexual orientation.

Instructions

The term sexual orientation refers to the preference one exhibits in terms of sexual partners. There is increasing evidence that one's sexual orientation is genetically-based; that is, sexual preference may be 'hard-wired' into the individual, and therefore resistant, if not impossible, to change. Other beliefs attribute early experience to later sexual preference. Regardless of the explanation you are most comfortable with, in your role as an educator you will encounter situations that will require your action and intervention on behalf of a child, either in making accurate attributions concerning a child's behavior at a given moment, or on behalf of a child who is experiencing strained relationships with her or his peers.

How would you explain the following scenarios to the concerned individual?

a. Four-year-old Jeremy heads right to the doll corner as soon as he arrives at the day care center each morning. His father is concerned that this behavior is not appropriate for a little boy. How would you respond to the father?

_____

_____

_____

_____

_____

_____

_____

b. Seventeen-year-old Patricia (who prefers to be called Pat) wears her hair cut very short and tends to dress like the boys. You walk by a group of her female classmates and hear them refer to her as a lesbian. How would you respond to this group of girls?

_____

_____

_____

_____

_____

_____

_____

_____

_____

_____

c. Five-year-old Suzanne plays with blocks and trucks during most of her free time in kindergarten. Her mother asks you if this is 'normal' behavior? How would you respond to the mother?

_____

_____

_____

_____

_____

_____

_____

_____

_____

_____

_____

d. In addition to his theater performances, thirteen-year-old Robert takes bal-
   let classes three days a week after school. Other boys often ridicule him in
   class. He comes to you and asks you to intervene. What would you suggest to Robert?

   _____

   _____

   _____

   _____

   _____

   _____

   _____

   _____

   _____

   _____

   What would you say to the other boys in Robert's class?

   _____

   _____

   _____

   _____

   _____

   _____

   _____

   _____

   _____

   _____

e. Fifteen-year-old Shauna, who has few friends, lifts weights and seeks out all the opportunities she can to play typical boys sports. She has also been having conflicting and confusing sexual feelings. She comes to you after school one day, initially to seek your advice about what to do about friends, but soon begins to talk about her confusion and fear of talking to her parents. What advise would you give her?

_____

_____

_____

_____

_____

_____

_____

_____

_____

f. Sixteen-year-old Joseph's stated goal in life is to become a nurse. You overhear a group of boys teasing him and laughing about his 'gay' behavior. You find Joseph sulking in a corner of the room and approach him. What do you say to him?

_____

_____

_____

_____

_____

_____

_____

_____

_____

Reflect upon your responses to the above scenarios. Do you notice any patterns in the way you answered the questions? Did you respond differently to the scenarios involving girls than you did for the scenarios involving boys? Did you respond differently to parents than you did to the child? If so, to what do you attribute this?

_____

_____

_____

_____

_____

_____

_____

_____

_____

_____

_____

_____

_____

_____

_____

_____

_____

_____

_____

_____

_____

The Student with Special Needs

Purpose

To assist future teachers with gaining greater understanding and insight into the probable expectations and responsibilities toward children with special needs.

Instructions

Full inclusion of all children in all classrooms is likely to be a major emphasis in the years to come, thus making it essential that all teachers are well-versed in ways to accommodate the needs of children with special needs. The following exercises will assist you in developing a greater understanding of your role and responsibilities.

A. Arrange to do an observation of a classroom that has children who have special needs. What do you notice about the manner in which the teacher interacts with the children who have special needs compared to those without special needs? What needs do the children seem to have that are unique to this group? Common to other children? What modifications in instructional approach are evident?

_____

_____

_____

_____

_____

_____

_____

_____

_____

_____

B. Interview a parent of a child who receives special educational services. In what ways has the child been helped? What improvements are still needed in the education the child receives? What recommendations does the parent have for you, as a future teacher, regarding what you might provide for children who have special needs?

_____

_____

_____

_____

_____

_____

_____

_____

_____

_____

C. Interview a teacher, focusing on how she or he has been affected by educational policy directed at children with special needs. What modifications has the teacher made in teaching? What special preparation has she or he received to help make the necessary changes? What does the teacher still feel is needed?

_____

_____

_____

_____

_____

_____

_____

_____

_____

_____

D. Ask to observe a conference where an Individual Educational Plan (IEP) is developed for a student with special needs. Analyze the perspectives and needs of each of the parties at the meeting. What concerns did parents address? Teachers? Administrators? Psychologists? Students? What concerns did you have that were not addressed?

_____

_____

_____

_____

_____

_____

_____

_____

_____

_____

_____

_____

Writing Your Own Critical Incidents

Purpose

To develop skill in writing critical incidents that can be used to instruct others about issues related to diversity in the school context.

Instructions

The critical incident is a short narrative describing a situation whereby two or more individuals from different cultural groups interact in order to achieve some goal. Differences due to cultural background, orientation, perspective, communication style, learning style, and so forth, may result in some conflict or problem emerging with the situation generally going unresolved. The reader is asked to select, from a number of alternatives, the one that best explains the problem. The general approach to preparing critical incidents is as follows:

1. Identify relevant themes or issues for your purposes. You may select from the 18-theme cultural-general framework, or identify specific issues of relevance to your needs. Remember, you wish to use the incident to teach others about a cultural issue or theme underlying the incident, not merely to relate the story.

2. Generate episodes by identifying incidents through personal experience, interviews with others, reading the research and/or ethnographic literature, or through observation and analysis. You may wish to use your observations from Activity 17 to form the basis of your incidents.

3. Construct episodes or stories, being certain to include only relevant information; verifying content; refining generalizations, abstractions, and specifics; and speaking to your intended audience. The resulting incident should be clear, concise, straightforward, interesting and believable, while maintaining the original conflict situation.

4. Elicit attributions, by identifying different interpretations (attributions) of the incident through interviews, ethnographic data, and by open-ended questions completed by experienced and inexperienced individuals.
5. Select attributions to use.
6. Complete the critical incident with feedback and explanations, remembering that it is in the explanation that relevant cultural knowledge can be transmitted.

Now, prepare three or four critical incidents that illuminate one or more of the 18 culture-general themes. Have the rough drafts of your incidents reviewed by others who provide critical feedback to make sure they are clear, plausible, and easily understood.

Activity and Reading 34

The Triad Model for Developing Multicultural Understanding

Purpose

To gain insight into how students from different cultural backgrounds might interpret statements made by teachers that ignore or contradict the cultural messages students bring with them to the classroom.

Instructions

One of the most difficult tasks to face teacher educators in recent years is that of preparing preservice teachers to work effectively with the diversity of students in their charge. The need to attend to human diversity in the educational process has never been greater, and educators have responded to this reality in a number of ways. Over the years we have witnessed the field of multicultural education advance from the mere addition of content through add-on courses, through attempts to develop more complex thinking, to more social action approaches designed to improve students' ability to transform the very processes and institutions in which they learn (Sleeter and Grant, 1987).

Yet, the knowledge base from which we draw the strategies and skills utilized to improve our understanding of and our interactions in the multicultural classroom and community is still in its infancy. In the search for effective means to reach these goals, some researchers and practitioners have attempted to apply concepts from the fields of cross-cultural psychology and training to improve teacher understanding and skill in working with diversity (Cushner and Brislin, 1986; Cushner, McClelland and Safford, 2003; Cushner, 1994a; 1994b). Such efforts have met with success in a number of contexts (Cushner, 1989; Cushner, 1990; Brislin, 1993). Thus, we are encouraged to continue to adopt and adapt materials and strategies that demonstrate potential and promise. This section presents an adaptation of the Triad Model of counselor training (Pedersen, 1977, 1988) to teacher preparation in a multicultural context.

Entering the Mindset of the Other: A Critical Skill

An essential element to the success in any relationship between teacher and student is the degree to which the student has allowed the teacher to enter into a coalition with her or him in the pursuit of learning. That is, unless a high degree of acceptance, understanding, and empathy between teacher and student has been established, the level of trust needed for a student to fully engage with the teacher will be insufficient. The greater the cultural difference between teacher and student, the less likely the teacher is to establish a meaningful and purposeful relationship in which to facilitate learning. The Triad Model of counselor training developed by Pedersen (1977, 1988) can serve as a model for providing training experiences for teachers as they prepare to work across cultures. Essentially, the Triad Model presents a counselor-training strategy that employs a three- or four-way interaction between the client, the counselor, and the problem from the client's perceptual worldview. We can adapt this model for use in teacher training.

Whenever a teacher and student communicate, there are at least three different conversations going on simultaneously. (For simplicity, let's begin by focusing on the interaction between a teacher and one student. However, keep in mind throughout this discussion that dialogue and interaction are occurring between a teacher and as many students as there are in the classroom.) At the objective or tangible level is the first dialogue, both verbal as well as nonverbal, that is going on between student and teacher. This is the most visible of the dialogues: the easiest to observe and analyze. In and of itself, this first dialogue is complex and fraught with numerous possibilities where cross-cultural differences do emerge. A second dialogue takes place in the mind of the teacher as she or he negotiates what was previously planned with the messages and observations made by the students. The skilled and reflective teacher continually adjusts his or her teaching according to the messages received and the manner in which they are interpreted. This second dialogue is internal and does not intrude in the first conversation. The teacher is able to monitor each of these two conversations. That is, the teacher can monitor what is being said or done in the course of teaching (the first dialogue) as well as attend to the thoughts and questions that occur within one's own mind as one reflects upon his or her own as well as upon the student's actions (the second dialogue).

However, there is a critical third dialogue or conversation that is going on during the teaching and learning process. This is the conversation going on within the mind of the student as she or he interprets what the teacher is trying to communicate. The student will think about alternative meanings to the messages the teacher sends as well as much irrelevant information that comes into the student's mind. The teacher does not know what this internal dialogue is about. The student, however, probably debates both positive (pro-teacher) messages as well as negative (anti-teacher) interpretations at all times—and responds accordingly. The Triad Model applied to teacher training is an attempt to make these positive and negative messages apparent to the teacher. As the teacher becomes better skilled at anticipating the internal dialogue of the student, she or he will be in a better position to make accurate adjustments in the teaching process.

As used in training, the Triad Model brings together a teacher and students for classroom instruction (as in a typical clinical or micro-teaching setting) along with two additional participants—the anti-teacher and pro-teacher. The role of the anti-teacher is to verbalize the negative internal dialogue that might be going on in the minds of the students, thus making it evident to the teacher. The role of the pro-teacher is to verbalize the positive internal dialogue that might be going on in the minds of the students, thus reinforcing those behaviors that facilitate learning. The Triad Model training session, one can imagine, can become quite noisy at times with talk going on by the teacher, responses from the students, as well as dialogue from the anti- and pro-teachers. Teachers working with students from different cultural backgrounds will have a difficult time understanding the internal dialogue accurately. With time and practice however, all engaged in the training process become better able to anticipate the messages that occur in the minds of the students, learn to make more accurate attributions or judgments about others, as well as plan more appropriate instructional experiences for students.

The Triad Model in Action

For the purposes of training, four roles are established: the teacher (T), who prepares and teaches a lesson typical of clinical experiences of most teacher-training programs; students (S), who assume the role of learner in the lesson; the anti-teacher (AT), who verbally points out verbal as well as nonverbal messages that might be in conflict with the students; and the pro-teacher (PT), who verbally identifies actions on the part of the teacher that are supportive and sensitive to the students and the instructional process. Through the course of the micro-teaching, the anti-teacher and pro-teacher continually verbalize positive and negative thoughts they anticipate the student might be making. The teacher should consider this dialogue and feel free to modify his or her teaching accordingly. While it takes a bit of practice, it is possible for participants to continue teaching and learning throughout the verbal onslaught.

An example of a simple Triad Model lesson in a fourth grade class follows:

T -   Good morning class. Today we're going to begin our unit on Thanksgiving. Who can think of some reasons why we celebrate Thanksgiving?

PT -   That's a good beginning. Try to involve the students right from the start.

AT -   Oh Yeah! Another great morning! I didn't have breakfast, again, and left the house late and angry at my mother. And this teacher just keeps on with her plans. I don't think she even thinks about my need for breakfast. Yeah! A great beginning!

S -   I'm thankful for my family.
        I'm thankful for my dog.
        I'm thankful we have a holiday coming up.

AT -   Here we go again! Teachers never consider the Native American children in the classroom and their perspective on Thanksgiving. There must be children all over the United States who each year have to put up with the discovery nonsense around Columbus and this so-called celebration of Thanksgiving. Why don't teachers understand that our ancestors were here long before theirs came? The Thanksgiving holiday continues to teach myths and stereotypes that we've known for years are wrong. Heck, it's not a day of celebration but a day of mourning for our people.

T -   Very good. Who can tell me what they know about the first meeting between the Pilgrims and the Indians?

PT -   Another good strategy, asking children to call upon their prior knowledge before really getting into the lesson.

AT -   And again. Let's drag up all those misconceptions from earlier years and keep them alive in the minds of children. When will teachers stop perpetuating these simplistic and distorted images designed to show how equitable the European settlers were? Everyone knows the Europeans abused the native peoples terribly for centuries. When will we stop telling lies about how cooperative everyone was?

S -   Pilgrims and Indians had a feast.
       They celebrated a harvest together.
       They celebrated the fact that they were neighbors.

T -   And what was served at the first Thanksgiving feast?

AT -   Why don't you ask what else besides food might have been there? What about a lot of apprehension, anxiety and uncertainty on both peoples' parts? Could people communicate well? Who did the translating? Or, I'll bet it was all in English — just the way Americans are today, assuming everyone speaks their language!

S -   Turkey and cranberries.
       Pumpkin pie and squash.

AT -   Why not teach the children the origins of the foods. Weren't most of the foods native to North America and introduced to the Europeans by the native peoples?

T -   Does anyone know where these foods originally came from?

Discussion

As can be seen in the above example, there are numerous anti-teacher messages that the student can make. But an effective teacher, once aware of potential pitfalls, can modify her or his actions accordingly as evident in the last line of the dialogue. In addition to the few issues brought out above, one can imagine the potential for gender inequity being raised in terms of teacher interactions; verbal and nonverbal messages being sent; the questions raised concerning the use of holidays and the predictable patterns that occur in the standard curriculum (i.e., studying the same African Americans each year and only in February), and so forth. But use of the Triad Model has the potential to bring out numerous other issues at play in the teaching-learning process as well. Issues of instructional methodology or strategy, especially as it relates to learning style preferences can be raised. Teachers can obtain feedback on their questioning strategies and discussion techniques, as well as how well they engage children's thought processes.

In using the Triad Model, students can read scripted role plays as the one above, or, can engage in the act of teaching a supportive group of peers who assume the various roles and help to point out the internal dialogue of the students. In addition, students might analyze already existing scripts of classroom interaction from the point of view of one particular group and predict where and under what circumstances teaching and learning might be affected by cultural differences.

Pedersen (1988) identifies numerous advantages of using the Triad Model in counselor training that apply equally to the teacher training context. The use of the anti-teacher offers individuals from one ethnic group the opportunity to role-play critical incidents likely to occur in the multicultural classroom in a safe and controlled setting. In addition, cross-cultural encounters are characterized by ambiguity, uncertainty, and are extremely abstract (Cushner and Brislin, 1996). The use of the anti-teacher helps to make cross-cultural problems and issues more concrete and less diffuse for the beginning teacher. Third, the anti-teacher can immediately identify inappropriate teaching techniques with direct and explicit feedback to the teacher education student by whatever means would be appropriate to the student's culture. Fourth, the teacher becomes more aware of the unspoken thoughts and feelings of the student from another culture and develops the ability to make more accurate judgments about others. Finally, the simulated classroom sessions can be videotaped and later analyzed in terms of specific ways in which cultural difference affect teaching and learning.

Activity

A. Prepare a script for a possible classroom scenario that illustrates the Triad Model in action. Use the script presented as a model for your scenario. Remember, your scenario should illustrate where issues of culture may interfere with the teaching and learning process and how they might be voiced in the mind of the student (and culture can be defined rather broadly to include references to gender, sexuality, social class, etc.).

B. The following exercise will require several steps and at least four people. The purpose of the exercise is to familiarize you with how the Triad Model works in the counseling relationship when participants act without prepared scripts.

1. Break into four-person groups.

2. Within each small group, each person will have the opportunity to role-play a counselor, client, procounselor, and anticounselor. As each person's turn to be the counselor comes up, the other three people will identify an area of 'shared cultural identity' among them that is not shared with the person in the counselor role. The area of cultural similarity may relate to ethnicity, nationality, religion, language, age, gender, place of residence, social status, educational status, economic status, sexual orientation, health or disability, and so forth.

3. The three-person team of client-procounselor-anticounselor will create a presenting problem based on their area of shared similarity with both a shallow (more obvious/overt) and a deeper (less obvious/covert) level to the problem.

4. The counselor will work with the three-person team for five to ten minutes, attempting to help the client manage the problem while getting feedback from the anticounselor and procounselor. The client will genuinely seek help with the problem. The anticounselor will articulate the client's negative internal dialogue. The procounselor will articulate the client's positive internal dialogue. There should always be at least two or three people speaking at the same time to adequately simulate the dynamics of the internal dialogue. Anyone may speak with anyone else during the interview.

5. After the interview, the participant should go out of role to discuss the interview process and content.

6. At the end of the discussion, participants should change roles and repeat the process until everyone has had an opportunity to experience each role.

part three

Modifying Curriculum and Instruction to Address the Goals of Diversity

Go to www.mhhe.com/cushner4e and click on *Human Diversity in Action* for a listing of Web Links.

Future's Window

Purpose

To project the needs of individuals and society in the years ahead, and to examine what this means for educators.

Instructions

In this activity you are to become a futurist and project into the future — both your own as well as that of the world. This page is divided into quadrants, the top half representing "The Self" and the bottom half representing "The World." The left side of each half represents "5 years" while the right half represents "20 years" into the future. You are to make at least five entries in each quadrant; things you expect to have accomplished or to be dealing with in 5 years and in 20 years, and things you expect the world to be confronting, both in 5 as well as 20 years. Do this activity alone at first. If you are doing this in a group setting, after a short while, you may share your responses with others and compile a group list.

Self—5 years	*Self—20 years*
World—5 years	*World—20 years*

Questions to Ponder

Look closely at what is on your list, or, if you have done this activity in a group, look closely at the compilation. What messages seem to jump out at you as you look closely at the response patterns? Do not be surprised if quick responses do not emerge. Take some time to analyze the similarities as well as the differences in the columns. What generalizations seem to emerge?

_____

_____

_____

_____

_____

_____

_____

What questions do you have as a result of the generalizations you observed?

_____

_____

_____

_____

_____

_____

_____

It is not uncommon, as people analyze their responses, to say something like, "It seems as if things will be quite nice and easy for us as individuals but there will still be problems in the world." This is a critical observation. If you have not already made this observation yourself, please consider it for a moment. Does such a statement hold true for your responses to the above task?

Let's assume that you can safely make the same observation and statement given the responses on your list. What is the responsibility one has to others? Why do you think it is that, in general, people project their own future to be fine even when the rest of the world continues to face enormous problems and challenges?

_____

_____

_____

_____

_____

_____

_____

_____

_____

Discuss your responses to the above with others in a group. Do not be surprised if there is much disagreement over people's responses.

Next, look closely at your projections for the world. What generalizations seem to stand out as you analyze this information?

_____

_____

_____

_____

_____

_____

_____

_____

_____

_____

Which of the following statements can you agree with given the projections you have made for the world? Check one.

_____ The issues that the world will face seem quite pessimistic and insurmountable.

_____ The issues that the world will face seem complex but generally will be resolved.

It is often said that each individual can and must do her or his own part to help improve the bigger picture. All of the problems the world will face, whether they are in fact solved or not, will require the coordinated efforts of many different people from many different backgrounds, both cultural as well as career, who are able to work together. The problems of the world are such that they will be solved by the coordinated efforts of many different people and nations, or they will not be solved at all.

What is the role of education in helping people develop the ability to solve the problems that you believe the world will face?

_____

_____

_____

_____

_____

_____

_____

_____

_____

_____

_____

_____

_____

What are some things you can do through your teaching that will help your students develop the awareness, knowledge, and skills necessary to collaborate with others whose ways of interacting and values may be quite different from their own?

_____

_____

_____

_____

_____

_____

_____

_____

_____

_____

_____

_____

_____

_____

_____

_____

_____

_____

_____

_____

_____

Using the Interpersonal Cultural Grid to Expand Intercultural Understanding

(adapted from Poterotto and Pedersen, 1993)

Purpose

To analyze behavior, both within and between two persons, so that intercultural conflict can be better understood and managed.

Instructions

Provide sample behaviors in each of the four quadrants below.

I	II
Identify examples where two culturally different individuals have similar behaviors and similar positive expectations (e.g., both expect friendliness and both smile)	Identify examples where two culturally different individuals have different behaviors but share the same positive expectations (e.g., both people expect friendliness but only one is smiling)
III	**IV**
Identify examples where two culturally different individuals have the same behaviors but have different expectation (e.g., both may appear friendly but may actually be in serious conflict. Or, both smile, but one wishes friendship and the other wants to sell you a car!)	Identify examples where two culturally different individuals have different behaviors and different expectations (e.g., likely to result in hostility and/or war).

1. Either individually or in small groups, suggest ways in which you can prevent the conflict in quadrant two from moving into quadrant three and/or four by not being distracted by culturally different behavior and emphasizing the shared and positive expectations between the two culturally different individuals.

_____

_____

_____

_____

_____

_____

_____

_____

_____

_____

2. If not already identified in the grid, think of some school-based examples of behavior that might fall into each of the four quadrants. Respond to question #1 above using these new school-based examples.

_____

_____

_____

_____

_____

_____

_____

_____

_____

Ethnic Literacy Test: A Cultural Perspective Differentiating Stereotypes from Generalizations

Purpose

To examine your knowledge of culture specific information about certain ethnic groups within the United States and how this might impact teaching and learning.

Instructions

Place a checkmark along the continuum that corresponds to the extent to which you agree or disagree with the following statements. Qualify your response in the space below.

Communication Differences

1. A newly-arrived Mexican American child may have difficulty in reading words that begin with two consonants.

strongly agree	tend to agree	unsure	tend to disagree	disagree strongly

Rationale:

_____

_____

_____

2. Non-standard English, such as Ebonics, is a language system that has rules.

strongly agree	tend to agree	unsure	tend to disagree	disagree strongly

Rationale:

_____

_____

_____

3. Many Appalachians form some possessive pronouns by adding n.

strongly agree	tend to agree	unsure	tend to disagree	disagree strongly

Rationale:

_____

_____

_____

4. Ebonics, sometimes known as Black English, is a synonym for Black slang.

strongly agree	tend to agree	unsure	tend to disagree	disagree strongly

Rationale:

_____

_____

_____

5. Vietnamese children may experience problems in spelling words that end with a double consonant.

strongly agree	tend to agree	unsure	tend to disagree	disagree strongly

Rationale:

_____

_____

_____

6. Vietnamese children would have little difficulty reading polysyllabic words.

strongly agree	tend to agree	unsure	tend to disagree	disagree strongly

Rationale:

_____

_____

_____

7. All Native Americans speak basically the same language.

strongly agree	tend to agree	unsure	tend to disagree	disagree strongly

Rationale:

_____

_____

_____

8. Touching by a teacher and a Mexican American student results in lowered academic achievement.

strongly agree	tend to agree	unsure	tend to disagree	disagree strongly

Rationale:

_____

_____

_____

9. Touching the head of a Thai student signals respect.

strongly agree	tend to agree	unsure	tend to disagree	disagree strongly

Rationale:

_____

_____

_____

10. African Americans may interrupt a speaker with encouraging remarks.

strongly agree	tend to agree	unsure	tend to disagree	disagree strongly

Rationale:

_____

_____

_____

Value Orientations

1. Native American concept of time is the same as mainstream European Americans' concept of time.

strongly agree	tend to agree	unsure	tend to disagree	disagree strongly

Rationale:

_____

_____

_____

2. Mexican American religious beliefs include the concept of fatalism.

strongly agree	tend to agree	unsure	tend to disagree	disagree strongly

Rationale:

_____

_____

_____

3. Appalachians have strong kinship bonds.

strongly agree	tend to agree	unsure	tend to disagree	disagree strongly

Rationale:

_____

_____

_____

4. African Americans have a strong work orientation.

strongly agree	tend to agree	unsure	tend to disagree	disagree strongly

Rationale:

_____

_____

_____

5. Native Americans usually prefer public rather than private recognition.

strongly agree	tend to agree	unsure	tend to disagree	disagree strongly

Rationale:

_____

_____

_____

6. Mexican American students generally desire to work alone rather than with a group.

strongly agree	tend to agree	unsure	tend to disagree	disagree strongly

Rationale:

_____

_____

_____

7. Appalachians adapt easily to urban life.

strongly agree	tend to agree	unsure	tend to disagree	disagree strongly

Rationale:

_____

_____

_____

8. African Americans tend to be deeply religious.

strongly agree	tend to agree	unsure	tend to disagree	disagree strongly

Rationale:

_____

_____

_____

9. For some African Americans, to avoid eye contact with authority figures is a sign of respect.

strongly agree	tend to agree	unsure	tend to disagree	disagree strongly

Rationale:

_____

_____

_____

10. Among Native Americans, the concept of private ownership is strong.

strongly agree	tend to agree	unsure	tend to disagree	disagree strongly

Rationale:

_____

_____

_____

Family Structures and Lifestyles

1. The African American family is matriarchal.

strongly agree	tend to agree	unsure	tend to disagree	disagree strongly

Rationale:

_____

_____

_____

2. The majority of Appalachian families are nuclear.

strongly agree	tend to agree	unsure	tend to disagree	disagree strongly

Rationale:

_____

_____

_____

3. The Appalachian family tends to be patriarchal, and boys are favored.

strongly agree	tend to agree	unsure	tend to disagree	disagree strongly

Rationale:

_____

_____

_____

4. Most Mexican American families represent the extended family pattern.

strongly agree	tend to agree	unsure	tend to disagree	disagree strongly

Rationale:

_____

_____

_____

5. Family roles are very specific and rigid in African American families.

strongly agree	tend to agree	unsure	tend to disagree	disagree strongly

Rationale:

_____

_____

_____

6. The Native American concept of family is similar to that of mainstream European Americans.

strongly agree	tend to agree	unsure	tend to disagree	disagree strongly

Rationale:

_____

_____

_____

7. Mexican American families are patriarchal.

strongly agree	tend to agree	unsure	tend to disagree	disagree strongly

Rationale:

_____

_____

_____

8. For most Native Americans and Asians, youths are honored and revered.

strongly agree	tend to agree	unsure	tend to disagree	disagree strongly

Rationale:

_____

_____

_____

Stereotype and Generalizations

Because people cannot respond to each and every piece of information to which they are exposed they form categories as an attempt to simplify the world around them. **Stereotypes** refer to categories about people. Categories in general, and stereotypes in particular, are shortcuts in people's thinking. As with most stereotypes applied to individuals, much of the content is inaccurate. We must, thus, be careful not to form stereotypes about people where they may not already exist.

Generalizations, on the other hand, can be useful in our thinking and interacting with others. **Generalizations** refer to trends over large numbers of individuals (Brislin, 2000). For example, if 100 cases were studied in collectivist and individualistic societies, more collectivists would behave in a manner that emphasized their group's goals, and more individualists would behave in a manner that emphasized their own personal goals. The concept of *trends over large numbers of people* is important to keep in mind whenever culture and cultural differences are discussed. We can use generalizations that are supported by the research literature in our discussions about culture, but should avoid the use of stereotypes.

The following are generalizations that can be made from the *Ethnic Literacy Test*. The responses you will read are generalizations that can be supported in the research literature. One must keep in mind, however, that there will always be cases that do not conform to the generalization and will make discussions more fruitful and engaging. Extend the response to these generalizations by suggesting some implications for education that are related to the specific information presented.

Communication Differences

1. Newly-arrived Mexican American children *may* have difficulty reading words that begin with two consonants. When compared to Standard English, the Spanish language has relatively few consonant clusters.

    Possible educational implications:

    _____

    _____

    _____

    _____

2. Non-standard English dialects, like Ebonics, are language systems that operate by rules. While the rules may be different, both standard and non-standard forms of a language operate by rules.
    Possible educational implications:

    _____

    _____

    _____

    _____

3. Many Appalachians form the possessive pronoun by adding "n," such as his'n or her'n.
    Possible educational implications:

    _____

    _____

    _____

    _____

4. Ebonics, or Black English, is *not* a synonym for Black slang. Ebonics is a dialect of Standard English which, like any language or dialect, has its own slang.
    Possible educational implications:

    _____

    _____

    _____

    _____

5. Since the double consonant is not common in Vietnamese language, Vietnamese children may experience problems in spelling words that end with a double consonant.
    Possible educational implications:

    _____

    _____

    _____

    _____

6. As the Vietnamese language is largely monosyllabic, Vietnamese children would tend to have difficulty learning to read polysyllabic words.
   Possible educational implications:

   _____

   _____

   _____

   _____

7. Native Americans do not all speak the same language — there are more than 400 different languages spoken by the people of the many distinct Nations.
   Possible educational implications:

   _____

   _____

   _____

   _____

8. Touching by a teacher and a Mexican American student may result in increased academic achievement as it signals affection and a strong relationship to the child.
   Possible educational implications:

   _____

   _____

   _____

   _____

9. Touching the head of a Thai student should not be done. The head is considered the most sacred part of the body and may signal the release of the spirit if touched.
   Possible educational implications:

   _____

   _____

   _____

   _____

10. African Americans *may* interrupt a speaker with encouraging remarks. Such is the basis for what is commonly referred to as *call and response*, and should not be misjudged as rudeness.
    Possible educational implications:

    _____

    _____

    _____

    _____

Value Orientations

1. The concept of time for many Native Americans may be quite different from that of European Americans.
   Possible educational implications:

   _____

   _____

   _____

   _____

2. Mexican American religious beliefs include the concept of fatalism, the belief that God controls much and if something is meant to be, God will make it happen. The individual may, thus, perceive him or herself to have relatively little control over a given situation. In Arabic, the phrase "N'Shalah" (if God wills it) captures this belief.
   Possible educational implications:

   _____

   _____

   _____

   _____

3. Appalachians tend to have strong kinship bonds.
   Possible educational implications:

   _____

   _____

   _____

   _____

4. Based on statistics from the Bureau of Labor Statistics, African Americans tend to have a strong work orientation.
   Possible educational implications:

   _____

   _____

   _____

   _____

5. Native Americans tend to prefer private rather than public recognition.
   Possible educational implications:

   _____

   _____

   _____

   _____

6. Mexican American students generally prefer to work in groups rather than as individuals.
   Possible educational implications:

   _____

   _____

   _____

   _____

7. Appalachians have a relatively difficult time adapting to urban life.
   Possible educational implications:

   _____

   _____

   _____

   _____

8. African Americans tend to be deeply religious.
   Possible educational implications:

   _____

   _____

   _____

   _____

9. For some African Americans (as well as some other groups), to avoid eye contact is a sign of respect.
   Possible educational implications:

   _____

   _____

   _____

   _____

10. Among Native Americans, the concept of private ownership is not common.
    Possible educational implications:

    _____

    _____

    _____

    _____

Family Structures and Lifestyles

1. The African American family tends to be equalitarian. That is, mothers and fathers tend to share responsibilities and roles fairly equally.
   Possible educational implications:

   _____

   _____

   _____

   _____

2. The majority of Appalachian families follow an extended family pattern.
   Possible educational implications:

   _____

   _____

   _____

   _____

3. The Appalachian family tends to be patriarchal with boys being favored.
   Possible educational implications:

   _____

   _____

   _____

   _____

4. Most Mexican American families represent the extended family pattern.
   Possible educational implications:

   _____

   _____

   _____

   _____

5. Family roles can be rather flexible in African American families.
   Possible educational implications:

   _____

   _____

   _____

   _____

6. The Native American concept of family follows the extended pattern.
   Possible educational implications:

   _____

   _____

   _____

   _____

7. Mexican American families tend to be patriarchal. That is, the father's decision is usually the final say.
   Possible educational implications:

   _____

   _____

   _____

   _____

8. For most Native Americans and Asians, the elderly tend to be honored and revered.
   Possible educational implications:

   _____

   _____

   _____

   _____

Determining Bias in Textbooks

Purpose

To develop skill in identifying stereotypes and bias in textbooks.

Instructions

Select a school textbook or other children's book that was printed many years ago. Using the guidelines below, evaluate the book for stereotypes of women, men, various ethnic groups, the elderly, and so forth. Repeat this exercise with a newer textbook and compare your findings.

Title of book: _____ Year of publication: _____

Give a brief description of the book:

_____

_____

1. Analyze the illustrations for stereotypes. What are people doing that may create or perpetuate a stereotype?

   _____

   _____

   _____

   _____

2. Analyze the storyline. What is the role of women or people of color in the story? How are problems presented and resolved?

   _____

   _____

   _____

   _____

3. Look closely at the lifestyles depicted in the book. How are different groups shown?

_____

_____

_____

_____

4. What people seem to have power in the book or story? Who is subservient? How are family relationships and composition represented?

_____

_____

_____

_____

5. From the reader's point of view, are there issues or norms that might limit or restrict one's aspirations or self-esteem?

_____

_____

_____

_____

6. What cultural, social and economic biases of the author might be evident?

_____

_____

_____

_____

7. Look for certain loaded words that might bias the reader. Are there words with derogatory connotations or overtones?

_____

_____

_____

_____

Now, repeat the exercise with a more recent book designed to achieve a similar goal. What differences are evident? To what would you attribute these differences? What cautions or concerns remain from your point of view?

_____

_____

_____

_____

_____

_____

_____

_____

_____

_____

_____

_____

_____

_____

_____

_____

_____

_____

_____

_____

_____

_____

_____

_____

_____

Rewriting Textbook Material to Reflect Diversity

(Adapted from Goldstein, 2000)

Purpose

To apply your knowledge and insights about cultural diversity to existing textbook material so they become more inclusive.

Instructions

Undoubtedly you have seen examples in textbooks where information related to diversity is marginalized; that is, it may be placed in the margins of the text, shaded in blue, or added at the end of a chapter. Your task will be to move such content from the margins to the main body of the text, or to add an appropriate dimension if it is missing. Select a 3 to 5-paragraph portion of a school textbook for a grade level or subject area in which you are preparing to teach. Rewrite the material so that it is more inclusive of research and/or approaches related to multicultural education.

An example of an inclusive rewrite of a college-level developmental psychology text that does not marginalize different groups is provided below.

Original

Baumrund's (1971) research indicates that parents generally employ one of three socialization patterns: authoritarian, permissive, or authoritative socialization.

Cultural influences included but marginalized

Baumrund's (1971) research indicates that parents generally employ one of three socialization patterns: authoritarian, permissive, or authoritative socialization. However, these patterns may not apply to all ethnic groups.

Inclusive rewrite

Research focusing on members of nuclear families, such as Baumrind's (1971) study of European American parents, has identified three main socialization patterns: authoritarian, permissive, or authoritative socialization. Studies addressing extended families as Chao's (1994) study of Chinese Americans, have found parenting styles that emphasize training children to know what is expected of them.

Make a copy of the portion of a textbook you will modify. On a separate page, demonstrate your ability to rewrite the portion while highlighting the modifications you have made. Your modifications should expand the text material so that it is more inclusive and reflective of the diversity of American society.

Learning Styles

Purpose

To analyze learning style differences among students and explore how they impact the classroom.

Instructions

Read the content below and respond to the questions that follow.

Learning styles are generally considered to be the cognitive processes and instructional settings a student finds most useful and effective while learning. Examples of such cognitive processes on a global scale include coding and decoding, organizing, perceiving, remembering, and reasoning (Hughes and More, 1993). The five most commonly recognized dimensions of learning that are found in the classroom (IBE, 1994) are:

a. **Global-Analytical**. Students who are more global learn best when the overall concepts are presented first, or presented in a meaningful context. Students who are more analytical tend to learn better when information is presented in small pieces and then gradually build up to an overall picture.

b. **Verbal-Imaginal**. Verbal learners tend to learn better from highly verbal explanations or from dictionary-like definitions. These students rely more on words and labels, use verbal regulation of behavior more effectively, and code concepts verbally. The more imaginal learners learn better from images, symbols, and diagrams.

c. **Concrete-Abstract**. Some students learn better when the concept is presented first in its abstract form, perhaps as a rule or principle. Others learn best when the concept is presented in its real form and as it will actually be used. This dimension is sometimes referred to as in-context versus out-of-context teaching and learning (Cushner, 1990).

d. **Reflective-Trial/Error/Feedback**. The reflective learner thinks through the new learning before actually using it. In the Trial/Error/Feedback style, the learner responds more quickly (trial), knowing the answer may not be correct (error), expecting to learn from the teacher's feedback to the response. One learns to ride a bicycle, for instance, using this method.

e. **Modality**. This reflects the fact that some students learn more effectively through seeing, others through hearing, others through touching, and so on.

Each of the above-mentioned learning style preferences can be individual or cultural manifestations. The important thing is that teachers are aware of the differences and that they become skillful at modifying their classrooms to accommodate the various needs or preferences of their students. Consider the next activity.

Listed below are a few differences in people's ways of thinking and interacting.

Thinking Patterns: The thinking patterns favored by a culture determine, to a great extent, the way people in that culture learn and teach. Consider some of these contrasting differences.

Analytic Pattern	*Global Pattern*
Operates with facts and data	Operates with ideas
Concerned with immediate results	Concerned more with the process
Highly analytical	Holistic or relational
Works well individually	Works well with others

What might be some of the consequences for students of the differences listed above?

_____

_____

_____

_____

_____

What are some of the consequences for educators given that they might have a classroom full of students whose learning styles preferences may include all of the above?

_____

_____

_____

_____

_____

What modifications in instruction might facilitate learning for students in each category? Your response should consider such aspects as pacing, experiential versus didactic presentations, as well as assessment and motivational strategies.

Global-Analytical

_____

_____

Verbal-Imaginal

_____

_____

Concrete-Abstract

_____

_____

Reflective-Trial/Error

_____

_____

Modality

_____

_____

Activity   and   Reading   41

The Goals of an Education that Reflects Diversity

Purpose

To understand the broad goals of diversity and examine them in terms of existing curricula.

Instructions

Read and discuss the following Goals of an Education That Reflects Diversity.

Over the years, numerous theoreticians and practitioners have proposed various definitions and goals for multicultural education. As expected, these statements have evolved as the field itself has broadened and redefined itself. The following attempts to integrate many of the various goals of multicultural education. The approach and some of the subsequent activities are modifications of a model developed by Davidman and Davidman (1994).

Goal 1

Improve understanding of the concept of pluralism in American society. Pluralism in this context must consider such sources of cultural identity as nationality, ethnicity, race, gender, socioeconomic status, religion, sexual orientation, health, and ability/disability (the attributes of culture identified earlier). One must look particularly at how each of these has impacted upon the individual as well as upon the group.

Goal 2

Expand the knowledge base of culture and the many different groups found in the United States (or any country) as well as abroad. At a content level, this considers curriculum inclusion of previously marginalized groups (e.g. women, people of color) as well as expansion to address multiple perspectives (e.g. racism in practice). At a process level, this considers pedagogical and communication processes.

Goal 3

Improve intergroup as well as intragroup interactions. This demands attention to such issues as cross-cultural understanding and interaction, attribution as well as assessment across groups, and conflict management. Teachers, thus, must broaden their instructional repertoire so that it reflects an understanding of the various groups that one will teach. Students must learn to communicate effectively across groups as well as develop the skills of collaboration that are needed for group problem-solving whether within or between groups.

Goal 4

Empower action-oriented, reflective decision-makers who are able and willing to be socially and politically active in the school, community, nation, and world. This goal is not only concerned with developing the knowledge and skill of practicing teachers but is also concerned with transferring this knowledge and skill to the pupils in their charge. Thus, individuals become proactive teachers and reflective practitioners who can ultimately prepare reflective citizen-actors, both of whom are able and willing to work for change in an interdependent world.

Discussion Questions

What do you interpret *each* of these goals to mean? Either in writing or in small groups, discuss the meaning of each of these goals.

Goal 1

_____

_____

_____

_____

Goal 2

_____

_____

_____

_____

Goal 3

_____

_____

_____

_____

Goal 4

_____

_____

_____

_____

How do you think *each* of these goals might be addressed in a variety of content areas (i.e., math, science, social studies, etc.)? Be as creative as you can as you consider how these goals might be put into action.

Goal 1

_____

_____

_____

_____

Goal 2

_____

_____

_____

_____

Goal 3

_____

_____

_____

_____

Goal 4

_____

_____

_____

_____

Modifying Existing Instructional Material to Reflect the Goals of Diversity

Purpose

To apply the four Goals of Diversity to a range of educational material, including existing lesson or unit plans.

Instructions

The goals stated in the previous activity can be easily put into practice in most content areas. One can, for instance, review a particular lesson or unit plan, paying particular attention to how each of the goals can be addressed. Each of the goals can be turned into a question that teachers are able to address in a given lesson or unit. Use the following as a guide. Then, you will be provided with a few examples of how lessons that utilize this approach might be developed. Finally, you will be asked to modify a lesson of your own.

1. How can the content and strategies of this particular lesson or unit improve student understanding of the concept of pluralism in American society while improving educational equity?
2. How can the content and strategies of this particular lesson or unit expand the knowledge base of culture and the many different groups found in the United States as well as abroad? Is the content accurate, inclusive, and free of bias? Does it give the whole picture? Does it strive to reduce or correct racist impressions?
3. How can the content and strategies of this particular lesson or unit improve intergroup and intragroup interactions? Are assessment strategies broad and inclusive? How is collaboration built into the activity? How can group harmony be improved?
4. How can the content and strategies of this particular lesson or unit empower action-oriented, reflective decision-makers who are able and willing to be socially and politically active in the school, community, nation, and world?

Following are four examples of lesson or unit plans that have been modified to consider the above goals.

(developed by C. Jeffrey Dykhuizen)

Lesson One
The Sense of Taste: Addressing the Goals of Diversity

The following is an example of how a typical science lesson on the sense of taste can be modified to address the goals of diversity.

....

Favorite Flavors and the Individual

Following the completion of a rather typical lesson that asks students to 'map' the tongue and identify where the taste buds for sweet, salty, bitter, and sour are located, engage students in a discussion of their favorite foods. To facilitate processing of the lesson, ask students where on their tongue they would be most likely to taste the flavor of their favorite food (i.e., ice cream would most likely be tasted on the tip of the tongue).

Find out by a show of hands how many have a favorite food that is sweet; sour; bitter; salty. What taste do most students prefer? Have students hypothesize why they think this might be.

Ask students if they have ever eaten a very delicious, bitter food. A stupendous sour food. A scrumptious salty food. Where? When? What?

Are students' favorite foods completely and exclusively one of the four major flavors, or a combination of flavors? What is their strongest preference? Their favorite combination? Are there other flavors that students identify other than the four given in the lesson? Is spicy a flavor?

Multicultural Taste Extension

Discuss the foods of different countries and cultures. Do certain cultures seem to emphasize different flavors in their cooking? Have students discuss why they think certain groups of people prefer certain flavors.

Extend the lesson by asking how many of the students like pickles. How do pickles taste? Are they sweet or sour? Can they be both? What are the various combinations of tastes that go into the flavor of a pickle? Where would you taste this on your tongue?

Goal 1: Explain the nature and evolution of pickles as a means to preserve foods. Nearly all cultures make pickles of some form or another. Discuss the various types of pickles students can find in their local food store. Can foods other than cucumbers be pickled? Other vegetables? Grains? Meats? What pickled foods did various immigrant groups bring with them to the Americas? What pickled foods were common to the indigenous groups in the Americas?

Goal 2: Compare the tastes of varieties of pickles. It may be best to initially compare the tastes of various pickles purchased at the local store (i.e., sweet cucumber pickles, dill pickles, mixed hot pickles, etc.).

Next, bring out pickles from different cultures. Japanese pickled plum or radish, Korean kimchi and German sauerkraut should provide good contrast. Explore reasons why a particular type of pickle is common to a particular culture. Discuss the geography of the country/culture in which that pickle is found. Which types of pickles do students prefer? Dislike? Why? Which type of pickle was most like ones they had eaten?

Goal 3: In small groups, have students analyze a variety of pickles. Which pickles are mostly sweet? Sour? Have students bring in samples of pickled foods found in their home and community. Have students explain why their own family prefers certain pickled foods. Have students discuss why they think humans have a sense of taste. What survival purposes must this have served? Do all humans have the same sense of taste? Why do they think certain cultures prefer certain tastes?

Goal 4: Have students analyze the impact on health due to pickles. Do all people consider them a healthy food? For instance, some consider pickled foods to be too high in sodium content. What considerations must be made when eating pickled foods? What changes have been evident in various societies with regard to foods that are high in sodium?

Are there certain pickled foods that you would like to see served in your school cafeteria? Available in area stores? How might you go about making your wishes known?

(developed by Jacqueline M. Szemplak)

Lesson Two
Human Diversity and the Human Figure

The following is a lesson extension of a sculptural art project studying the human figure from a diverse perspective. The lesson can be used with middle and secondary level students.

....

The following extension has been modified from an art lesson dealing with the human figure. Instead of studying the human figure solely from a Western perspective, students will see examples of sculptures from other areas of the world. As an introduction to the lesson, students will write down their personal thoughts and beliefs on what they consider to be beautiful in a sculpture. What attributes would it have? What type of dress might it have, if any? What would its proportions be? What would be the overall mood of the piece? Would it look like anyone they know, or any famous piece of artwork? Students might generate their own list.

As a multicultural extension, students would view examples of figural sculptures from different time periods and different cultures around the world. Some examples might include Mayan, Egyptian, West African, Japanese, ancient India, and any of the many multicultural modern American sculptures. Then, in small groups and using the list they made earlier, students will discuss which of these sculptures best fits their description of beauty. Will they need to change or modify their original ideas? What do they believe was the intent of each artist? What are the various reactions of viewers of each piece? What elements reflective of the culture are evident in the piece? What materials were used to create the piece? Then, as an entire class, students should construct their universal list of characteristics they believe should be evident in a piece of sculpture. Eventually, they will use their own criteria as a guideline to make and evaluate their own sculptures.

Goal 1: Students will analyze how their own culture views the human figure and discuss why and how they were ingrained with a Western view of art. They can discuss how art serves as a form of identity for a culture, subculture, or ethnic group. Forms of art examined may be political, gender-related, religious, or another form that reflects a particular time period or social context. Students should discuss the social and political impacts that Western art forms have had on them.

Goal 2: The teacher should guide the students to define the human figure and beauty from a multicultural perspective. This can be accomplished by viewing a variety of sculptures from around the world. Students should come to realize that beauty is culturally defined and that it varies from culture to culture. While not all of the sculptures viewed will be considered beautiful by the criteria of Western art, students should understand that each are considered beautiful and may hold deep cultural meanings in the cultures in which they were created.

Goal 3: Students will improve intergroup relations by working cooperatively in groups. They will discuss their own views of figural sculptures as well as the views of others in their class. They will collectively refine the ideas of sculptural beauty from a multicultural perspective. They will then work in small groups to create a sculpture that reflects the criteria they have decided upon.

Goal 4: When the small groups have completed their sculpture, they will share them with the entire class. What considerations should be made while viewing each sculpture? Would all people define this as good artwork? Why? Is it museum quality, or might it be considered folk art? Why? What is its best quality? What changes would you want to see if you were a museum curator? How would you make your wishes known? How might you encourage others to view figural sculpture from other ethnic or cultural groups?

(developed by Kim Elliott)

Lesson Three
Diversity in the Animal Kingdom

The following multicultural lesson extension suitable for the early years illustrates how a science lesson might be used to introduce the concept of diversity. While this lesson specifically targets bears as the animal of focus, it can easily be modified for other animal species. The following extension has been prepared with kindergarten children in mind.

....

Most kindergarten teachers in my district do a brief unit on bears, without addressing the "real" aspect of the animals. Teachers tend to use bear stories and stuffed animals to approach the unit, and integrate a variety of arts-and-craft-type activities to engage children. This may be fine to introduce the lesson and perhaps to personalize it, but time on this aspect could and should be kept to a minimum. Children might be asked if they have a favorite bear as a lead-in to the lesson, but they should then concentrate on the more "real" aspects of the animal, as well as on the diversity of bears and how it might relate to humans. Here is one way in which this might be accomplished.

Goal 1: Read a story about bears and ask children where they might be able to see a bear. Ask if all bears at the zoo look the same. Why don't they all look alike? Ask children if they think all bears come from the same place? Discuss with children that even though there may be many different kinds of bears, they are each unique and special in their own way. Show pictures of different types of bears, and have children point out the obvious similarities and differences (e.g., size, shape, color, etc.).

Goal 2: Use books and various photos to show children that bears do not all come from the same place. It is here that a teacher might begin to introduce a globe or map while discussing different environments in which bears are found. Have children attempt to match pictures of different bears to a variety of environments and suggest why they think a certain bear might be found in a particular region. You may use a variety of bears and locations, such as the panda from China, the polar bear from the arctic, and grizzly bears from mountainous regions. Note that the koala from Australia is *not* a bear. This might be introduced early in the unit, and children can explore why people tend to classify it as such. This might be used as an example of stereotyping at a later time.

Goal 3: Have the children work in groups to draw the environments from which several bears have originated. Have them share their pictures as a group with the rest of the class. Discuss with the children the different types of foods that each bear eats. Explain that the reason the bears eat these different types of foods is that they are naturally occurring in the environments in which they live (e.g., panda-bamboo, polar bear-fish, grizzly-fish). Bring in samples of bamboo and fish for the children to examine. Which of these foods would they eat? Why? Why not? Have them consider if people in these parts of the world eat similar foods. Why? Why not? Discuss that just as bears' eating habits differ from region to region, so, too, do the eating habits of people who live in different regions.

Goal 4: Bring together all the different ideas children have been discussing. Discuss with children that just as there are different types of bears in the world, there are also different types of people. Also discuss that like the bears, people from different parts of the world live in different environments, eat different foods, and enjoy different types of activities. Using the bears as parallels to humans, go back to the original idea of the unit to explore that we are all humans, are all unique and special, even if we come from different parts of the world.

As an extension, let the children plan an imaginary trip to one of the regions to see their favorite bear in its natural environment. During the trip, you might study such things as the region's geography, climate, native peoples, and foods.

(developed by Kaleroy Zervos)

Lesson Four
The Diverse World of Birds

The following might be a supplement to a unit on birds for elementary grades that integrates the goals of diversity. Throughout the unit ask the children how the actions and nature of birds can be related to the actions and nature of people.

Goal 1: As the students determine which birds are common to their local area, ask them why only these birds seem to be in this part of the country. Are they found anywhere else in the country? In the world? Why are some birds only found in certain areas? Why aren't ostriches native to their area? Are these birds always here or do they migrate? Why do birds migrate? Can all birds fly?

Ask students to consider the different groups of people that live in their region. Did these groups always live there? Are there groups of people native to their region? Are there any similarities between the reasons animals migrate and the reasons people migrate?

Goal 2: As the students begin to note which birds eat which foods, have them examine which birds eat the same foods. Do ground-feeding birds have a preference different than the post-feeding or tree-feeding birds? Ask students to contemplate why some birds eat on the ground and others from a post or tree. Do different people eat differently (i.e., eating utensils, chairs vs. cushions, etc.)? Do people who eat differently eat the same foods? Why might these differences exist?

As students determine the pecking order of birds, ask them to examine why the pecking order is structured the way that it is. Are some birds larger than others? Why might the birds at the top of the pecking order scare the others away? Is it possible that they like to eat alone, or do they simply want more food? How can we be sure we know why the birds at the top of the pecking order scare the lower birds away? Can we be sure? Could there be more than one reason?

Ask students to examine if there is a pecking order on the playground, such as on the swings or concerning the use of certain equipment. Do the older children "scare" the younger children away from certain equipment? Do we know why? Can we be sure as to why? Could there be more than one reason? How might we find out?

Goal 3: Throughout the unit the students work together. When they build bird feeders, for instance, each group must determine how they are going to build the structures, what materials they will need to build them, and how they are going to set them up. The students also work together on such things as bulletin boards and other displays.

Students also consult one another on their procedures and progress. Especially when checking for fright distance, for instance, students must watch one another to determine how close they can get to the birds before they fly away. They must also determine how they will record and present the results of their observations.

Goal 4: The students can become empowered in many different ways through such a unit. They can develop and execute their own procedures (i.e., building bird feeders to determine pecking order) and so forth. As they gather information through their observations and through research, they can share their information with others in the class. Students might attempt to determine changes in bird populations over the years and suggest programs to stabilize or help to return endangered species to the area.

Applying the Contact Hypothesis to Improve Intergroup Relations

(Adapted from Goldstein, 2000)

Purpose

To apply criteria from the contact hypothesis to improve intergroup relations in schools

Instructions

It has become increasingly clear that merely putting students from differing backgrounds together in the same environment does not necessarily guarantee positive outcomes or an improvement in intergroup relationships. Gordon Allport proposed the contact hypothesis, elements found to be critical to bringing different groups together and reducing prejudice, as far back as 1954. Research conducted over the years continues support his original hypothesis, albeit with a few provisos. Relations between students from different racial and ethnic groups are most likely to result in a reduction of prejudice when the following conditions are met:

- individuals are on equal status with one another (economic, social or task-related), implying that they have equal access to any rewards available in a given setting (resources, grades, participation in extra-curricular activities);
- students interact with one another on a repeated basis while in pursuit of some common task;
- students have the opportunity to get to know one another as individuals, thus interacting with a wide range of people who disprove the prevailing stereotypes of the group; and,
- the efforts are sanctioned by administrators and others in authority.

Contact may actually increase prejudice in circumstance where the contact:

- reinforces any pre-existing stereotypes;
- leads to competition between groups;
- is forced, imposed, or unpleasant;
- is between people of unequal status.

Read the following scenario and answer the following questions based on the contact hypothesis.

Mrs. Martin teaches a 10th grade Language Arts class that is comprised of 27 students; approximately equal numbers of African American, European American, Latino/a and Asian Americans. The majority of the European American and Asian American students come from a similar, middle socioeconomic background and attended the same middle school. The majority of the African America and Latino/a students attended a different middle school that tends to serve those in a lower socioeconomic neighborhood. In most situations in Mrs. Martin's class, the different groups self-segregate by ethnic group and rarely interact with one another in the classroom. While the students tend to sit with their own group when given a chance, there are times when Mrs. Martin asks them to work together in interethnic groups on various projects. The students typically resist these efforts, sometimes with outright hostility.

1. What might be some of the underlying causes of any intergroup hostility that may develop?

_____

_____

_____

_____

_____

_____

_____

_____

_____

2. What steps might you take to improve the situation in the class described above?

_____

_____

_____

_____

_____

_____

_____

_____

_____

_____

3. Relate a school-based experience that you are familiar with involving students from different groups that was problematic. How might you apply the contact hypothesis to improve the outcome?"

_____

_____

_____

_____

_____

_____

_____

_____

_____

_____

_____

Activity 44

Now It's Your Turn: Modify a Lesson to Address the Goals of Diversity

Purpose

To apply the *Goals of Diversity* to a lesson you develop.

Instructions

Select an already prepared lesson plan for the subject area you plan to teach. Or, develop your own lesson or unit plan. Review this lesson with the four goals in mind, and respond to the questions as stated below.

1. How can the content and strategies of this particular lesson or unit improve student understanding of the concept of pluralism in American society while improving educational equity?

   _____

   _____

   _____

   _____

   _____

2. How can the content and strategies of this particular lesson or unit expand the knowledge base of culture and the many different groups found in the United States as well as abroad? Is the content accurate, inclusive, and free of bias? Does it give the whole picture? Does it strive to reduce or correct racist impressions?

   _____

   _____

   _____

   _____

   _____

3. How can the content and strategies of this particular lesson or unit improve intergroup and intragroup interactions? Are assessment strategies broad and inclusive? How is collaboration built into the activity? How can group harmony be improved?

_____

_____

_____

_____

_____

_____

_____

4. How can the content and strategies of this particular lesson or unit empower action-oriented, reflective decision-makers who are able and willing to be socially and politically active in the school, community, nation, and world?

_____

_____

_____

_____

_____

_____

_____

Creating Cross-Cultural Understanding Through Internationally Cooperative Story Writing

Social Education 56(1).
1992, pp. 43–46, ©
1992 National Council
for the Social Studies
Reprinted with permission

The following article presents the Partnership Story Project, an activity designed to link classrooms in different parts of the world or nation through a joint story-writing project. Read about how a classroom of children in Ohio collaborated with a classroom of children in India to write and illustrate a story that was then presented in both the English and Tamil languages. Then, consider how you might use the story-writing process as a means to connect with classrooms around the world, the nation, or within your own region. What benefits would you expect to derive from such an activity?

by Kenneth Cushner*

Culture learning and culture teaching are two critical skills teachers and students must develop to live effectively in today's world What, exactly, we mean when we speak of culture learning, and just how we develop this skill, has been the subject of investigation among social psychologists and cross-cultural trainers for over three decades. Elementary schools have begun to pay attention to this concept only recently.

Those working in the field of cross-cultural training find it useful to distinguish between objective and subjective dimensions of culture (Triandis 1977; Cushner and Trifonovitch 1989). Objective culture generally refers to the tangible, visible products of a given people. Subjective culture, on the other hand, refers to the invisible, less tangible aspects of a group of people, such as their values, norms of behavior, attitudes, and worldview; the things people generally carry around in their minds. Subjective dimensions of culture are much more difficult than the objective dimensions to analyze, investigate, and discuss with others, in part because they are generally kept secret even from oneself (Cushner and Trifonovitch 1989). Good cross-cultural training recognizes that

* The author wishes to thank Ms. Sandi Goodrich, 4th grade teacher at Walls Elementary School, and S. Jayapragaram, Department of Gandhian and Ramalinga Studies, Kamaraj University. in Madurai, India for their assistance with this project.

it is at the level of people's subjective culture that most cross-cultural problems occur. This, then, should be the focus of educational efforts.

Cross-cultural trainers have developed a range of strategies designed to help individuals understand critical aspects of another culture and thus improve intercultural understanding (Brislin, Cushner, Cherrie, and Yong 1986). The strategies that have proven most effective on people's knowledge, affect, and behavior appear to be cognitive approaches that effectively engage the emotions. That is, cross-cultural training strategies that go beyond mere information giving to engage students actively in developing empathy or an insider's view of another culture have a greater effect on people's perceptions and behavior.

The following project—well-suited to the school context—may serve to increase student understanding of the subjective elements of culture. This one-of-a-kind project integrates cooperative learning strategies and involves active participation of young people in developing a common product with peers overseas. The Partnership Story Project, an internationally cooperative story-writing project, resulted in increased international understanding and culture learning by elementary schoolchildren in northeastern Ohio schools and their peers in India, Mexico, Hungary, Norway, and the Soviet Union. This article relates the process and results of one such effort designed to integrate whole-language learning and the social studies.

The Partnership Story Project

The story is a timeless and age-old cultural medium for exploring human imagination, values, and conflicts. Parents and Teachers for Social Responsibility of Moretown, Vermont, started the Partnership Story Project in 1989 in an attempt to bring young people from two countries together for collaborative story-writing projects. Through such projects, groups of children in one country begin writing and illustrating a story of special interest to them. This story is developed to a point of climax and then sent to a group of similar-aged schoolchildren overseas who complete the story. The participating children present a complete, illustrated story in both languages.

Partnership Stories work on many levels to engage children in learning about themselves and the world around them. In addition to receiving a part of a story and accompanying drawings (if desired by the classroom teacher), the project participants can hear their counterparts' voices on cassette tape, share photographs, or exchange brief personal biographies, songs, messages of goodwill, and so forth. Through such activities, children enhance their cultural and geographical awareness; explore social, economic, and environmental questions of the time; engage their imagination and cooperation in group problem solving, both in their own classroom and with children overseas; gain confidence to act in a positive manner toward and with others in their world; and develop international friendships.

Following is a story cowritten by 4th grade children of Walls Elementary School in Kent, Ohio, and similar-aged children in N. M. R. Subbaraman Memorial Residential Primary School in Madurai, India. Walls school is a predominantly white, middle-class neighborhood school close to the campus of Kent State University in northeastern Ohio. Twenty-five students participated in the development of the first part of the story. Madurai is located in the southernmost region of India As the head teacher of the school in Madurai writes:

> This is a special school run by Tamilnadu Harijan Sevak Sangh (a state branch of a national non-governmental organization) which was originally found[ed] by Mahatma Gandhi for the uplift of the untouchables. The school admits only the children of scavengers (who are the lowest in the economic and social status within the untouchable group) and they are the first generation of children in their group to enter formal schooling. The children enjoyed this task. Their creativity is revealed in these pages. I was deeply moved by their creativity. The children convey their gratitude and joy and hope to see this project in its completed form.

Nine students and three teachers together wrote the end of the story.

Following is the story, "A Jungle Adventure," written and illustrated by these two groups. I have indicated where the U.S. children stopped writing and sent the story to the participants in India to finish. At that point, stop and ask yourself how you think the story will end. After you learn how the children from India completed the story, you might reflect upon what you think you have discovered about their way of life. Summaries of the U.S. students' responses to hearing the ending will be presented.

Part One

Once in a circus there was a tiger who would not perform because he was lonely. The circus owner sent his daughter, Maryetta, to the jungle to find a friend to perform with the lonely tiger. Maryetta's father gave her $1000 to purchase a tiger. Her father told her to spend the money wisely.

The next day on a boat trip to the jungle, Maryetta met a trapper named Toby.

Toby asked Maryetta, "Why are you going to the jungle?"

Maryetta replied, "I am traveling to the jungle to purchase a tiger for my father's circus."

"What a coincidence," Toby said, quickly figuring out a way he might obtain Maryetta's money before the real trapper could reach her. "I am meeting a girl from a circus tomorrow!"

"You are?" Maryetta asked, looking puzzled. "Do you know what circus she is from?"

"No," replied Toby, "but it must be yours. How many girls could there be going to the jungle tomorrow to buy a tiger?"

"I guess you're right. I'll meet you by the river at 10:00 tomorrow morning."

Toby wanted to get there before the real trapper did, so he said, "Why don't we meet at 9:00 and get an early start?"

This they agreed to and then went their own ways.

The next day was a beautiful summer day, perfect for trapping tigers. Toby rented a boat and met Maryetta precisely at 9:00.

"I'll need to collect my fee of one hundred dollars each morning before we begin," Toby told Maryetta.

"I thought you told my father your fee was one hundred and fifty dollars per day," Maryetta said' wondering why he had lowered his fee.

"Oh, well I guess I forgot what I said before. One hundred and fifty dollars it is then," said Toby.

"Alright, but I don't have a lot of money. Do you think we'll be trapping for a long time?"

"Probably only two or three days," Toby reassured

"Well, then, let's get going!" exclaimed Maryetta.

At first, the boat trip down the river was pleasant. About noon, however, the boat struck a huge rock which punctured its side. The rest of the day Maryetta and Toby spent repairing the boat. As a result, they had to spend the night on the river bank.

During the night, Maryetta thought she heard voices. When she peeked out of her tent she saw Toby talking to a wolf. She couldn't believe her eyes or ears! Although she had been raised around the circus and always knew that animals were special, she had never talked to one! She listened intently.

"Go make friends with the tiger and bring him back here," Toby told the wolf.

"When do you want me to bring that stupid tiger back?" asked the wolf.

"Five days from now will be good. Then I will have enough money to buy the secrets I want from that old wizard."

"Okay. See you then," said the wolf, and he crept away.

Maryetta silently closed the flap of her tent and slumped to the ground. Something was very, very wrong. How was she going to get back to the circus safely with the tiger and not let Toby know she knew he was a fake?

The next morning Toby told Maryetta the boat was fixed

Toby then said, "I don't want to be rude, but where is my money?"

Maryetta answered, "I'll pay you later." She thought to herself, I have no intention of paying Toby.

Toby said, "I want my money now!"

Maryetta said that because the boat accident was not her fault she should not have to pay for the first day.

Toby replied, "Well, it's not my fault either, and besides, we had an agreement."

They argued for a while and Toby finally agreed that Maryetta could pay him later. He told her he would begin to look for the tiger today.

They boarded the boat together to begin the search for the tiger. Along the way they spotted a beautiful tiger being chased by a wolf.

Maryetta said, "Toby, I know you sent the wolf after the tiger and you better make sure the wolf doesn't harm him or you won't be paid!" They anchored the boat and went ashore.

Toby and Maryetta began to chase after the tiger and the wolf. Suddenly, Maryetta tripped over a vine and broke her leg. Toby came along, grabbed Maryetta's money, and ran off with it!

This completes the first part of the story. This portion was sent to India where the children decided upon, and wrote, an ending through a similar cooperative process. Before reading how the Indian children completed the story, ask yourself how you would complete the story. What major events would you have happen to resolve the situation presented in the story as it stands now?

Before reading the ending, the U.S. children were asked the very same question. Of the twenty-five children who responded ten carried the story to completion in such a manner that Maryetta's task was fulfilled. In these cases, Maryetta catches the tiger, takes it home, and it performs as desired in the circus. Three students resolved the problem by creating a new character who comes to the rescue and saves Maryetta from her injury and from Toby. In six cases, the tiger frees Maryetta from her crisis and in three of these the tiger goes on to catch Toby. In two cases, Maryetta escapes, finds the wizard, and seeks revenge on Toby. In one case each the wolf helps Maryetta catch first the tiger and then Toby; Toby steals the money from Maryetta and does not catch the tiger; Maryetta is cured in a hospital and becomes friends with Toby; and Toby spontaneously recognizes and reconciles his evil ways.

Part Two

The wolf who was chasing the tiger stopped after hearing Maryetta's cries and ran toward her. He finally reached her. He felt sad when he saw the flow of blood from her leg.

"Don't be afraid. I shall help you," said the wolf.

The wolf then ran into the forest and brought rare herbs and placed them on her legs. At once, Maryetta felt relief from the pain and felt pleasant again. Maryetta looked at the wolf with love and gratitude.

The wolf asked Maryetta, "How did you fall?"

She explained everything to him. The wolf felt bad when he heard of Toby's treacherous deeds. The wolf told Maryetta that he would get the money from Toby.

Maryetta saw the birds, trees, and other creatures around her. Suddenly she didn't feel lonely any more. She felt happy that she was part of an endless creation of nature. She felt the encouragement and nourishment given by the surrounding birds and trees.

Toby went straight to the old wizard with the money he robbed from Maryetta. After getting the money from Toby, the wizard taught him the mantras (magic phrases) which he could use to conquer the animals and humans. Toby then quickly left, greedy to make money.

Then, Toby saw a tiger running towards him in a frenzy. He tried to conquer the tiger with the mantras he had leaned from the wizard. But the tiger pushed him down and tried to attack him. At that time, the tiger heard the voice of a wolf and he ran away.

The wolf and Maryetta saw Toby struggling for his life. The wolf did not like to help the treacherous Toby. He thought that this was the right punishment for his terrible deeds. But Maryetta was deeply moved by Toby's suffering. She felt sad that she did not have the money to admit him into a hospital.

Maryetta pleaded with the wolf to help Toby. The wolf halfheartedly ran and brought rare herbs. Maryetta made a bandage with the herbs for Toby's wounds. She also gave him some juice from the herbs. He then recovered and could breathe easy again.

Toby slowly came to consciousness and appreciated the gentle qualities of Maryetta and apologized to her. He revealed that he had given the money to the old wizard. He felt sorry that he was spoiled by his own greed.

In the meantime, the wolf went to the tiger. He asked the tiger, "Why did you try to kill Toby?"

The tiger angrily replied. "It is but natural that we are angry towards men who prevent us from living independently in the forest and who try to hunt us. Toby is trying to destroy us totally by violence, tricks, and mantras. For him, money is bad."

The wolf said, "Toby not only cheats the animals, but also the humans. For this greedy fellow, money is everything."

Toby was truly sad. He felt ashamed of himself and asked to be pardoned. Then the wolf, the tiger, Toby, and Maryetta danced together in a circle.

Then Maryetta told the tiger, "In my father's circus there is a male tiger suffering without a companion. If you can come with me, he would be very happy."

Maryetta looked at the female tiger with love and affection The female was moved to tears. She began to wonder if that male tiger was the one that had been taken away from her long ago. She agreed to go with Maryetta

All four returned to the circus. The male tiger was happy to see the female tiger that he had been separated from so very long ago. Soon they were able to identify one another. What a pleasure it is when separated ones come together again!

Maryetta was very happy. She had learned to talk with the animals. Her love toward them grew many times over. She looked after the tigers with special care.

One day Maryetta fell asleep while laying with the tigers. She listened to the conversations of the tigers as she woke up. She pretended as if she was sleeping and continued to listen to them.

The female tiger said, "Maryetta is a wonderful girl. But she does not realize that the forest is our heaven. Even this golden cage is still a cage." Maryetta was deeply moved. The next lay Maryetta's father called her and said, "Maryetta, I have grown old. I am retiring from the circus as of today. Hereafter, you should run the circus"

Maryetta said, "I shall free those wonderful animals from this sorrowful, tortuous caged life and I will go and live in the forest."

And that she did.

In what ways is this ending different from the one you expected? What surprised you as you read the story? What do you think you learned about Indian culture? What does reading this story teach you about U.S. culture? These are the same questions asked of the U.S. children immediately after hearing how the Indian children completed the story. This type of inquiry presents a tremendous opportunity for culture leaning to occur.

For the most part, the U.S. children were surprised that good would prevail over evil. The majority of respondents (fifteen of the twenty-five) commented that they did not expect the bad characters to change for the good. This might suggest that they are surprised by the idea that the human personality is inherently good and that it is malleable and can be changed by sudden insight, spontaneous experience, or reflective thought. Six children were surprised that all the characters went to live in the forest together. Three were struck by the use of herbs and mantras in the story. For one student, the fact that all went to the circus seemed most startling.

Asking these 4th graders to reflect upon what they learned about Indian culture was a bit more difficult. Of the sixteen children who responded to this question, seven suggested that Indians care about nature in general and animals in particular; six suggested that Indians might desire all people to be good, safe, and peaceful (not to suffer or struggle); and one each hypothesized that Indians are caring people ("because bad guys can become good"), that they care for people, and that herbs and mantras are an "important part of life" for them.

Even fewer children were comfortable responding to what they thought they learned about U.S. culture; with encouragement and greater structure, this dimension might be expanded. Two children felt that people in the two countries were probably alike in many ways (they did not, however, expand upon what this meant), two were surprised that we (in the United States) would let the characters in the story struggle and die (obviously responding to their own expectations of how the story would end); one thought that perhaps people in the United States do not treat animals very well; one suggested that the United States is a violent society; and another suggested that once someone is labeled an enemy, that label might stay with them for some time.

Standing on its own, and without much teacher guidance, it appears that children are able to extract a significant amount of culturally relevant information from the body of a story. Subsequent classroom activities related to teaching about India might now be linked to this motivational activity and the personal relationships and understandings that have been developed between these children.

Other possibilities certainly exist with such a project. The way this project was carried out, we could not determine how many different endings the Indian children might have generated. In and of itself, this would be of considerable interest; that is, how much variation might there be from the ending they provided? What kinds of difficulties, learnings, obstacles, and so forth, were evident among the Indian children? One might ask what kinds of assumptions were made on the part of the U.S. storywriters that might be troublesome for the Indian children. For instance, is the wolf or tiger an appropriate key figure in a story? What about the fact that a girl was the central character and was ultimately given responsibility for the circus? What other possibilities might exist that could become problematic? What did the Indian children learn about U.S. culture by reading the beginning of the story? How would the U.S. children have completed a story started by the Indian children?

While it can be quite difficult to identify a school overseas and ultimately carry out such a project, significant learning might also occur by having children within one country complete a Partnership Story. Improved understanding, interactions, and relationships could be developed between diverse groups in the United States through such an effort. For example, how might stories develop between children in inner-city schools and those in nearby suburbs? Between children on reservations and in nearby areas?

At this time the only groups carrying out such projects are Parents and Teachers for Social Responsibility in Moretown, Vermont, and undergraduate preservice teachers at Kent State University. Teachers interested in participating in and receiving guidelines for conducting such a project, both in this country and abroad, are encouraged to contact the Vermont group or me.

Increasingly, educators are being asked to integrate an international and intercultural perspective into their curriculum. Integrating strategies that demonstrate significant influences in cultural learning, and especially in helping individuals develop greater understanding of subjective levels of culture and its effects on behavior, will become increasingly important. An approach such as the Partnership Story Project can effectively serve these goals.

Inventory of Cross-Cultural Sensitivity

©Kenneth Cushner, 1986

Purpose

To complete a self-assessment instrument with regard to your intercultural experiences.

Instructions:

The following questionnaire asks you to rate your agreement or disagreement with a series of statements. Please respond honestly as there are no correct answers. You can now compare your responses from the beginning of the book.

Please circle the number that best corresponds to your level of agreement with each statement below

	1 = Strongly Disagree 7 = Strongly Agree
1. I speak only one language	1...2...3...4...5...6...7
2. The way other people express themselves is very interesting to me	1...2...3...4...5...6...7
3. I enjoy being with people from other cultures	1...2...3...4...5...6...7
4. Foreign influence in our country threatens our national identity	1...2...3...4...5...6...7
5. Other's feelings rarely influence decisions I make	1...2...3...4...5...6...7
6. I can not eat with chopsticks	1...2...3...4...5...6...7
7. I avoid people who are different from me	1...2...3...4...5...6...7
8. It is better that people from other cultures avoid one another	1...2...3...4...5...6...7
9. Culturally mixed marriages are wrong	1...2...3...4...5...6...7
10. I think people are basically alike	1...2...3...4...5...6...7

	1 = Strongly Disagree 7 = Strongly Agree
11. I have never lived outside my own culture for any great length of time	1...2...3...4...5...6...7
12. I have foreigners to my home on a regular basis	1...2...3...4...5...6...7
13. It makes me nervous to talk to people who are different from me	1...2...3...4...5...6...7
14. I enjoy studying about people from other cultures	1...2...3...4...5...6...7
15. People from other cultures do things differently because they do not know any other way	1...2...3...4...5...6...7
16. There is usually more than one good way to get things done	1...2...3...4...5...6...7
17. I listen to music from another culture on a regular basis	1...2...3...4...5...6...7
18. I decorate my home or room with artifacts from other countries	1...2...3...4...5...6...7
19. I feel uncomfortable when in a crowd of people	1...2...3...4...5...6...7
20. The very existence of humanity depends upon our knowledge about other people	1...2...3...4...5...6...7
21. Residential neighborhoods should be culturally separated	1...2...3...4...5...6...7
22. I have many friends	1...2...3...4...5...6...7
23. I dislike eating foods from other cultures	1...2...3...4...5...6...7
24. I think about living within another culture in the future	1...2...3...4...5...6...7
25. Moving into another culture would be easy	1...2...3...4...5...6...7
26. I like to discuss issues with people from other cultures	1...2...3...4...5...6...7
27. There should be tighter controls on the number of immigrants allowed into my country	1...2...3...4...5...6...7
28. The more I know about people, the more I dislike them	1...2...3...4...5...6...7
29. I read more national news than international news in the daily newspaper	1...2...3...4...5...6...7
30. Crowds of foreigners frighten me	1...2...3...4...5...6...7

	1 = Strongly Disagree	7 = Strongly Agree

31. When something newsworthy happens I seek out someone from that part of the world to discuss the issue with   1...2...3...4...5...6...7

32. I eat ethnic foods at least twice a week   1...2...3...4...5...6...7

Scoring the ICCS

The ICCS can be scored by subscales. Simply insert the numbered circled on the test form in the spaces provided under each subscale heading. Reverse the values for the items marked with an asterisk (*) . For instance, reverse scoring results in:

7=1, 6=2, 5=3, 4=4, 3=5, 2=6, 1=7

Then, add the values in each column for the subscale score. A total ICCS score is obtained by adding the various subscale scores together. Individuals can be ranked relative to others in a particular group. You can also identify relative strengths and weaknesses that may lead to more focused orientation and planning.

ICCS Scoring Guide   Subject ID_____

C Scale		B Scale		I Scale	
item	score	item	score	item	score
1*	____	2	____	3	____
6*	____	7*	____	8*	____
11*	____	13*	____	14	____
12	____	19*	____	20	____
17	____	25*	____	26	____
18	____	30	____	31	____
23*	____				
24	____				
29*	____				
32	____				

A Scale	E Scale	
item	score	item
4*	____	5*
9*	____	10
15*	____	16
21*	____	22
27*	____	28*

Totals

C Scale = ____

B Scale = ____

I Scale = ____

A Scale = ____

E Scale = ____

Total ICCS Score = ____

* Reverse score all items marked with * as these are negatively worded items.

Interpreting the Inventory of Cross-Cultural Sensitivity

The ICCS is a 32-item instrument composed of five subscales that provides dimensional scores for individuals on each subscale. Individuals can be ranked relative to others from high to low levels of sensitivity on issues and experiences related to cross-cultural or intercultural interaction (the higher the score, the more sensitive an individual is presumed to be). Results of such an inventory are of potential interest to those who need to identify individuals best able to undertake an international or intercultural transfer or those best able to adjust to the demands of cross-cultural personnel changes (e.g. desegregation efforts in schools); programs that desire to evaluate the impact of curriculum intervention and program experience; and for those wishing to simply raise people's awareness of some of the issues to consider prior to intercultural interaction.

The five subscales and the range of scores include:

Subscale	Range of Scores
Cultural Integration (C Scale)	10–70
Behavioral Scale (B Scale)	6–42
Intellectual Interaction (I Scale)	6–42
Attitude Toward Others (A Scale)	5–35
Empathy Scale (E Scale)	5–35
Total Score Range	32–224

Now, compare your results on each subscale with those when you first completed the inventory at the beginning of the book (see Activity 2).

What surprised you most when comparing your scores?

_____

_____

_____

_____

_____

In what areas have you shown the most growth? The least? To what would you attribute these changes (or lack of changes)?

_____

_____

_____

_____

_____

_____

_____

What questions or issues did this instrument fail to address that you believe would better demonstrate how you have grown or changed?

_____

_____

_____

_____

_____

_____

_____

The Technical Details of the ICCS (or the fine print)

Content validity looks to the extent to which a test encompasses a reasonable sample of the responses or behaviors that characterize the variable of interest. Thirty-two statements that effectively differentiated individuals varying in amount of intercultural experience, and which when factor analyzed using varimax rotation loaded highly on one dimension and maintained eignevalues greater that 1.0 were retained in this version of the ICCS.

Construct validity refers to the degree to which the instrument succeeds in measuring what it purports to measure. The ICCS has effectively differentiated individuals having extensive intercultural experience (two or more years living and/or working overseas) from those having little or no intercultural experience (undergraduate university students living in northeastern Ohio). Those having limited intercultural experience have ranked between these two groups. The ICCS has demonstrated the ability to differentiate individuals having received cross-cultural training from control group members (Broaddus, 1986; Cushner, 1989).

Reliability refers to the extent that the instrument obtains consistent and stable results. Reliability estimates for the ICCS appear to be quite stable: C Scale = .9415; B Scale = .7009; I Scale = .8869; A Scale = .7860; E Scale = .5239.

Glossary

Ambiguity: An unclear message. In the cross-cultural context this refers to the lack of clarity that typifies many interactions that still requires an individual to respond.

Anxiety: An emotional state of general and undefined nervousness that often exists in an intercultural encounter due to the unfamiliarity of another's behavior.

Attribution: The judgments people make about others based on the behavior they observe.

Belonging: The need people have to feel as if they have a role and purpose in a given setting or context.

Categorization: The process of dividing stimuli into classes or groups according to a particular system. In the cultural context, this refers to the manner by which one's culture teaches one to view the world around them.

Collective Group: Refers to members of a group that tend to identify with one another who will often be deferred to when making decisions.

Communication Differences: Generally refers to group-level differences in both verbal as well as non-verbal modes.

Differentiation: Refers to the process of distinguishing the finer points between elements of a given category, as a wine connoisseur is able to do. In the cross-cultural context, this refers to distinctions made between aspects of a category that are important to a given group of people.

Disability: Refers to the inability to do something that is desirable.

Disconfirmed Expectations: Refers to the tendency individuals may have that cause them to become upset or uncomfortable, not because of the specific circumstances they encounter, but because the situation differs from what they expect.

Ethnicity: Ethnicity refers to the knowledge, beliefs and behavior patterns shared by a group of people with the same history and the same language.

Ethnocentrism: The tendency people have to evaluate others from their own cultural reference.

Faulty attributions: Inaccurate judgments made about others. In the cross-cultural context this refers to judgments made by an observer using criteria that are not used by the particular actor in a given situation.

Fundamental attribution error: The tendency people have to judge others using different criteria that they would use to judge themselves.

Gender: Socially defined category in which the biological specialization of male and female are transformed by associating specific personality, role, and status traits to each sex.

Generalization: refers to the tendency of a majority of people in a cultural group to hold certain values and beliefs, and to engage in certain patterns of behavior. Thus, this information can be supported by research and can be applied to a large percentage of a population or group.

Group allegiances: Tendency to identify and make major decisions according to those preferred by a group to which one identifies, which can be ethnic, religious, national, etc.

Health: Health is culturally defined according to a particular group's view of what physical, mental, and emotional states constitute a "healthy" person. The "expert" opinion of the medical profession usually guides a view of health in the industrialized world, although alternative systems such as acupuncture, holistic medicine, and faith healing are available; the acceptance of which varies widely both within and between social groups.

Individual interests: Tendency to identify and make major decisions according to one's own individual preferences as opposed to those of the group.

Ingroups: Refers to those individuals one feels psychologically closest to and who often share rather intimate knowledge and interpersonal relationships.

Language: A collection of meaningful sounds used to communicate messages to others.

Learning style: a consistent pattern of behavior and performance by which an individual approaches educational experiences; learning style is derived from cultural socialization, individual personality, as well as from the broader influence of human development.

Model minority: Refers to those groups who excel in school and who appear to have overcome discrimination.

Nationality: Identification and the state of belonging to a particular nation-state.

Nonverbal communication: Means of communication that are unspoken and may or may not accompany verbal communication. Refers to such things as gestures, facial expressions, use of space, etc.

Objective culture: The visible, tangible aspects of a group of people, including such things as the artifacts produced, the clothing worn and food that is eaten.

Outgroups: Refers to those persons generally kept at a psychological distance from oneself.

Prejudice: Non-reflective judgments about others that are harsh, discriminatory, or involve rejection.

Privilege: A special advantage or right granted or enjoyed by certain individuals or groups.

Race: Biologically speaking, it refers to the clustering of inherited physical characteristics that favor adaptation to a particular ecological area. Race is culturally defined in the sense that different societies emphasize different sets of physical characteristics when referring to the concept of race. Thus, race is an important social characteristic, not because of its biology, but because of its cultural meaning in any given social group or society.

Religion: Religion is defined on the basis of a shared set of ideas about the relationship of the earth and the people on it to a deity or deities and a shared set of rules for living moral values that will enhance that relationship.

Rituals: A series of acts performed in a prescribed manner, usually in conjunction with a religious or spiritual ceremony.

Role-based behavior: Patterns of behavior expected to be carried out in a manner deemed appropriate for a given position one may hold.

Sexuality: Particular patterns of sexual self-identification, behavior, and interpersonal relationships that identify one as either male or female.

Situational behavior: Behavior of an individual or a group that is characteristic in a particular setting or context.

Social status: refers to the degree to which an individual has power, influence, or leadership in his or her social group.

Socialization: the process whereby individuals learn what is appropriate to be a functioning member of a particular group, such as family, work or social group.

Spirituality: Spirituality generally refers to a set of ideas about the relationship of an individual to the earth and to deities. Whereas religion is generally group-oriented and formal in its organzation, spirituality can refer to a more personal experience.

Stereotypes: beliefs about the personal attributes of a group based on the inaccurate generalizations used to describe all members of the group, thus ignoring individual differences.

Subjective culture: refers to the invisible, intangible aspects of a group, including such things as attitudes, values, norms of behavior; the things typically kept in people's minds.

Superstitions: A belief or practice resulting from ignorance or false conception of causality.

Values: Internalized beliefs that provide social cohesion among group members that are often codified into laws or rules for living, such as the Ten Commandments for Christians and Jews or the Hippocratic Oath for doctors.

References

Ah, but the mystery. Akron Beacon Journal, June 25, 2000, A 12.

Allport, G. (1954). *The Nature of Prejudice*. Reading, MA: Addison-Wesley.

Baumrind, D. (1971). Current Patterns of Parental Authority. *Developmental Psychology Monographs, 4(1, part 2)*.

Bellah, R.; Madsen, R.; Sullivan, W.; Swindler, A.; and Tipton, S. (1985). *Habits of the Heart: Individualism and Commitment in American Life*. New York: Harper and Row.

Berger, P. L. and Berger, B. (1972). *Sociology: A Biographical Approach*. New York: Basic Books.

Brislin, R. (2000). *Understanding Culture's Influence on Behavior, 2nd ed*. Fort Worth: Harcourt Brace Jovanovich.

Brislin, R.; Cushner, K.; Cherrie, C.; and Yong, M. (1986). *Intercultural Interactions: A Practical Guide*. Beverly Hills: Sage Publications.

Broaddus, D. (1986). *Use of the Culture General Assimilator in Intercultural Training*. Unpublished doctoral dissertation, Indiana State University, Terre Haute.

Center for Educational Statistics. *The Digest of Statistics*. Washington, D.C.: U.S. Government Printing Office.

Chao, R. K. (1994). Beyond Parental Control and Authoritarian Parenting Style: Understanding Chinese Parenting Through the Cultural Notion of Training. *Child Development, 65*, 1111-1119.

Chomsky, N. (1966). *Cartesian Linguistics*. New York: Harper and Row.

Cushner, K. and Brislin, R. (1986). "Bridging Gaps: Cross-Cultural Training in Teacher Education." *Journal of Teacher Education*. 37(6), 51-55.

_____ (1989). "Assessing the Impact of a Culture-General Assimilator." *International Journal of Intercultural Relations*. 13, 125-146.

_____ (1990). "Cross-Cultural Psychology and the Formal Classroom." In R. Brislin (Ed.) *Applied Cross-Cultural Psychology*, (pp. 98-120). Newbury Park: SAGE.

_____ (1992). "Creating Cross-Cultural Understanding Through Internationally Cooperative Story Writing." *Social Education.*, vol. 56, no. 1, 43-46.

_____ (1994b). "Cross-Cultural Training for Adolescents and Professionals Who Work with Youth Exchange Programs." In R. Brislin and T. Yoshida (eds.) *Improving Intercultural Interactions: Modules for Cross-Cultural Training Programs*. Newbury Park: SAGE.

_____ (1994a). "Preparing Teachers for an Intercultural Context." In R. Brislin and T. Yoshida (eds.) *Improving Intercultural Interactions: Modules for Cross-Cultural Training Programs*. Newbury Park: SAGE.

Cushner, K. and Brislin, R. (1996). *Intercultural Interactions: A Practical Guide, 2nd. edition*. Thousand Oaks, CA: SAGE Publication.

Cushner, K. and Trifonovitch, G. (1989). "Understanding Misunderstanding: Barriers to Dealing with Diversity." *Social Education*, vol. 53, no. 5, 318-322.

Cushner, K.; McClelland, A.and Safford, P. (2003). *Human Diversity in Education: An Integrative Approach, 4th edition*. New York: McGraw-Hill.

Davidman L. and Davidman P. T. (1994). *Teaching with a Multicultural Perspective: A Practical Guide*. New York: Longman

Drum, J., Hughes, S. and Otero, G. (1994). *Global Winners: 74 Learning Activities for Inside and Outside the Classroom*. Yarmouth, ME: Intercultural Press.

Gilligan, C. (1982). *In A Different Voice*. Cambridge, MA: Harvard University Press.

Goldstein, S. (2000). *Cross-Cultural Explorations: Activities in Culture and Psychology*. Boston, MA: Allyn and Bacon.

Gollnick, D. and Chinn, P. C. (1990). *Multicultural Education in a Pluralistic Society, 3rd edition*. New York: Macmillan.

Herek, G. M. (1986). "On Heterosexual Masculinity: Some Psychical Consequences of the Social Construction of Gender and Sexuality." *American Behavioral Scientist, 29*(5), p.5.

Hofstede, G. (1980). *Culture's Consequences: International Differences in Work-Related Values.* Beverly Hills: Sage Publications.

Hughes, P. and More, A. J. (1993). *Learning Styles/Patterns and Aboriginal Students.* Presentation to the World Conference on Indigenous People's Education. Wollongong, Australia, December 1993.

Ilola, L. (1988). *Intercultural Interaction Training for Preservice Teachers Using the Culture-General Assimilator with a Peer Interactive Approach.* Unpublished doctoral dissertation, University of Hawaii.

International Bureau of Education, (1994). *Educational Innovation and Information* (Sept., 1994). Geneva, Switzerland.

Kennedy, M.M.; Jung, R.; and Orland, M. (1986). *Poverty, Achievement, and the Distribution of Compensatory Education Services.* Washington, D.C.: U.S. Government Printing Office.

LeVay, S. and Hamer, D.H. (1994). "Evidence for a Biological Influence in Male Homosexuality." *Scientific American*, vol. 270, 44-49.

McIntosh, P. (1988). *White Privilege and Male Privilege: A Personal Account of Coming to See Correspondences through Work in Women's Studies.* Working Paper No. 189. Wellesley, MA: Wellesley College Center for Research on Women.

Pedersen, P. (1977). "The Triad Model of Cross-Cultural Counselor Training." *Personnel and Guidance Journal*, 56, 94-100.

Pedersen, P. (1988). *A Handbook for Developing Multicultural Awareness.* Alexandria, VA: American Association for Counseling and Development.

Ponterotto, J. and Pedersen, P, (1993). *Preventing Prejudice: A Guide for Counselors and Educators.* Newbury Park: SAGE Publications.

Root, M. P. (1998). Experiences and Processes Affecting Racial Identity development: Preliminary Results from the Biracial Sibling project. *Cultural Diversity and Ethnic Minority Psychology, 4,* 237-247.Samover, L.; Porter, R.; and Jain, N. (1981). *Understanding Intercultural Communication.* Belmont, CA: Wadsworth

Slavin, R. (1979). *Student Team Learning as a Total Instructional Program: Effects on Achievement and Attitudes*. Baltimore: Center for Social Organization of Schools, Johns Hopkins University.

Sleeter, C. and Grant, C. (1987). "An Analysis of Multicultural Education in the United States." *Harvard Educational Review*, 57(4), 421-444.

Summerfield, E. (1997). *Survival Kit for Multicultural Living*. Yarmouth, ME: Intercultural Press.

Triandis, H. (1972). *The Analysis of Subjective Culture*. New York: Wiley-Interscience.

Trifonovitch, G. (1977). "Culture Learning/Culture Teaching." *Educational Perspectives,* vol. 16, no. 4, 18-22.

Vonnegut, K. (1974). Afterword, in F. Klagsburn (Ed.) *Free to Be...You and Me*. New York: McGraw-Hill.